PRAYERS FOR THE PEOPLE

PRAYERS
FOR THE PEOPLE

*Things We Didn't Know
We Could Say to God*

TERRY J. STOKES

Convergent
NEW YORK

Published in the United States by Convergent Books, an imprint
of Random House, a division of Penguin Random House LLC, New York.

CONVERGENT BOOKS is a registered trademark and its C colophon
is a trademark of Penguin Random House LLC.

LIBRARY OF CONGRESS CATALOGING-IN-PUBLICATION DATA
Names: Stokes, Terry J., author.
Title: Prayers for the people / Terry J. Stokes.
Description: New York : Convergent, [2021]
Identifiers: LCCN 2021012918 (print) | LCCN 2021012919 (ebook) |
ISBN 9780593239438 (hardcover : acid-free paper) |
ISBN 9780593239445 (ebook)
Subjects: LCSH: Prayers.
Classification: LCC BV260 .S845 2021 (print) | LCC BV260 (ebook) |
DDC 242/.8—dc23
LC record available at https://lccn.loc.gov/2021012918
LC ebook record available at https://lccn.loc.gov/2021012919

Printed in Canada on acid-free paper

crownpublishing.com

2 4 6 8 9 7 5 3 1

First Edition

Book design by Fritz Metsch

To Eric, Danny, Mark, and Chris—
my first daily prayer partners

To the Trinity Fellows "class hot mess"—
my best friends in the world

To the wonderful youth of RCHP

CONTENTS

II: SINGLENESS AND ROMANCE

III: FAMILY AND HOME

IV: THE SELF

V: COMMUNITY AND SOCIETY

VI: WORK AND VOCATION

VII: RECREATION

VIII: MUSIC

IX: CHURCH LIFE

INTRODUCTION

I WAS RAISED in a church tradition in which the only way we prayed was extemporaneously. Any kind of prayer that was formal or pre-written—the handful of times that I would experience it at my grandma's house or a friend's church—struck me as rote, uninspired, and emotionally disengaged. If the words weren't coming directly from where my heart and mind and soul were at in that moment, the prayer was a less authentic reflection of me, and therefore less effective—or even counterproductive—toward my goal of developing an authentic relationship between Jesus and the real me.

This was definitely the case at the evangelical megachurch of my youth, but it reached its peak at the charismatic-adjacent Black church of my college years. Every Sunday we would enter the sanctuary in need of inspiration, and boy would our worship pastor take us there. He began each service with five to ten minutes of passionate off-the-cuff prayer, music ebbing and flowing behind his emotional swells, to the point where any resistance melted away, hearts fired up, and everyone was spiritually locked in—ready to sing and dance the house down. I miss those days.

The summer after I graduated from college, I went to work as the worship intern at a Presbyterian church in Charlottesville,

Virginia, as part of a one-year fellowship program. I can still viscerally remember the dread that I felt after my first Sunday there. I remember saying to myself, *Worship should not be scripted like this! How can you know what you're going to pray before the moment comes? Where's the openness to the move of the Spirit? Where's the room for spontaneity? I cannot do this for nine months—I already need a revival after one day! Alexa, play Kirk Franklin.*

But before a couple of months had passed, God had changed my heart, showing me how formal liturgy can be a much-needed protection against the "tyranny of the novel." I learned that worship does not have to be spontaneous, new, or unique in order to be faithful. There's immense beauty in our expressing ourselves to God out of the present state of our hearts and minds, but there's also power in the way God forms and shapes us through words that have been slowly and deliberately crafted by liturgists over the past week, or year, or generation, or even over the breadth of our traditions.

During my years at Princeton Seminary, I worked at a wonderful Episcopal parish on the Upper West Side of New York City (a fun Sunday morning commute), and later at St. Philip's, a historically Black Episcopal parish in Harlem. As I spent those three years saying the same collect for purity, the Nicene Creed, the Lord's Prayer, and various other unchanging parts of the liturgy, I learned that common prayer can open the door to deeper levels of engagement and internalization. Like the lyrics of an old favorite song, the words take up residence deep down in our souls. Every recitation "above the surface" draws from memories and associations that shoot out like roots beneath our conscious thoughts and words. This creates a level of buy-in that for me has felt like being drawn tighter into God's arms.

After I was confirmed into the Episcopal Church in early 2019, I started saying morning prayer daily at Trinity, the parish down the street from my apartment on campus. This meant that I was praying 1) with other people, 2) with roughly the same group of people each time, 3) at the same time five days a week, 4) in the same place. I would not have been able to unlock the solitude and silence of solitary evening prayer without having several months of the former under my belt first.

This also meant that, by the time I started doing evening prayer as well, I was doing a Psalm, Old Testament, Epistle, and Gospel reading each day according to a lectionary; and that I had discrete space for adoration, for confession, for thanksgiving, and for supplication. Adding this liturgical structure to my daily devotions created a routine that worked for me unlike anything I'd tried previously in my life.

The balance and variety of genres of Scripture and idioms of prayer, as well as the centering of the liturgy on the Psalms—the prayer book of the Bible—clicked for me in a way that reading through one book at a time, using popular devotionals, and other approaches hadn't. The fact that most of the liturgy followed repeated or rotating forms, and was more focused on participation than reflection, took the onus off of me to come up with the words or the feelings that would make my devotion "good" on any particular day (e.g., *I did morning prayer today and thereby offered my faithful attention and service to God* versus *I had a good quiet time this morning because I extracted this insight or felt that emotion*).

This was also my introduction to the kind of prayer called a "collect" (*KA-lict*, emphasis on the first syllable). A collect is a short written prayer that gathers up (or *collects*) similar prayer concerns, and articulates them in a broad, general way. Put differently, it crystallizes or condenses a variety of similar ideas into one prayer that, by virtue of its form and place in the prayer book, is something that an entire communion can lift up together. The Book of Common Prayer has collects for each week of the liturgical year, for various saints' days and other holy days, and, in the back, ones for various people, topics, or events (e.g., for monastics, for the right use of God's creation).

Later that year, I saw someone tweet out "a collect for when chips must be eaten quietly," formatted in the font and style of the Book of Common Prayer, which delighted me to no end. Combining a traditional form with contemporary experience through the rhetorical lens of humor? Genius! It was also the first time I considered that an average person could write their own collects, and even share them with others who might find them worth saving and using. The seed was planted.

A few months later, I had the opportunity to write my first collect for my parish's first celebration of the feast of the Reverend Peter Williams, our first rector and the second Black man ordained in the Episcopal Church. I enjoyed the experience of a new kind of writing, a new way of praying, and the way in which a private spiritual exercise could then be of service to others in a more public setting.

A few weeks after that I went on a first date, and, as I often do, I was getting way into my feelings way too quickly (e.g., planning my dance feature for the wedding reception, naming the kids, designing the house, etc.). But in an effort to grow as a person, I was determined to channel the energy in a more productive way this time.

So I decided to write a collect "for when one is enamored but must be chill about it" (see page 21).

As playful as it was, the collect was *genuinely* efficacious in many respects: it helped me invite God into my romantic life, and allowed me to channel my thoughts into productive acknowledgments and requests to God, rather than letting them run wild.

I texted the collect to a few friends, mainly just as a humorous peek into my life. Turns out, they all thoroughly enjoyed it, so I tweeted it, and folks enjoyed it there as well. Incentivized by the personal benefits and public interest, I decided to write one collect per day for the foreseeable future.

So began a solid stretch of several months where I would post my work daily: prayers for when one is getting trolled on the internet, for when one has been ghosted, for before opening a dating app, and so on. The project became a wonderful way to combine contemporary concerns with traditional language and form, and to bring into my ongoing conversation with God various parts of my life that had not previously been represented there. The response from Christian Twitter quickly grew beyond anything I'd imagined—it was almost as if folks were waiting for this kind of project to be put out into the world.

Six months pass, and like a good millennial, I was running an Instagram account. Lovely people were regularly sending me affirmations, or requests for prayers they would like me to write—a significant number of which made it into this collection. And some were reporting that they'd begun to write prayers of their own (which has been perhaps the most humbling outcome of this project for me).

Many folks have expressed to me that they are drawn to the juxtaposition of traditional language with modern concerns and vernacular, which gives the prayers a combination of transcendence and groundedness. I've also found that their humor and levity, striking in the context of formal prayer, make them all the more accessible and easy to internalize.

This year I've had folks request collects touching on eating disorders, anxiety, being Black at white or cross-cultural churches, deep longing for marriage and children, teaching, and so much more. I'm so grateful for those who have shared their hearts with me in this way. It's been first and foremost a wonderful way to give and receive care, and also a way to expand the scope and perspective of my work and make it more "common."

As the project grew, I began to dream of collecting the prayers in a book. Making them easier to reference, and more readily distributable, would be a big part of making them available for common prayer—that is, repeated communal use. The speed with which this dream became a reality still confounds me even as I am writing this. I am so grateful.

I've been overjoyed to see similar public prayer-writing being done (do check out @blackliturgies and @liturgiesforparents, for starters) by other lovely folks who are part of this ressourcement and liturgical renewal movement in the American church (especially its younger generations). With the books that I'm sure they'll be publishing, there will be a wave of resources coming out soon that will introduce or reintroduce folks to the beauty of common prayer, and I am pumped about that.

My number one hope for my work is to encourage others to

try the spiritual practice of prayer-writing for themselves. Here is a collect "recipe" that has enriched my prayer life, and that I commend to you:

1. Pick a title—what or who the prayer is for.
2. Begin the prayer with an address to God.
3. Continue with an attribute or action of God.
4. Content (what do you want to say to God about this?)
5. End with a Trinitarian doxology.
6. If you're above 120 words or so, see if you can trim it down.

You'll notice that each prayer in this collection follows this formula. They are divided into sections based on theme. I hope that these are words that you can touch and agree with, and offer up to God as individuals and as communities of faith. Grace and peace to you.

I

FRIENDSHIP

THE BASIC UNIT *of the church is not the family but the friendship. What is radical about the church is not the binding of people who are already tied by blood or marriage, but people who would otherwise have no tie at all.*

I wrote those words in my journal while reading Wesley Hill's *Spiritual Friendship,* which was not only a significant stepping-stone along my journey to affirming theology during seminary, but also an occasion for me to participate in the larger resurgence of attentiveness to friendship (and a corresponding de-emphasis of the nuclear family) that I've seen over the past few years in the church circles that I'm a part of.

I've struggled to find deep, consistent, present friendships in my short adult life. No doubt, I've found great friends in individual chapters of life, but I've often struggled to carry those relationships over to the next chapter. From college to a yearlong intentional community program, to seminary, to my current chapter as a youth pastor living alone in a new town, I've moved around quite a bit, and the answer to the question "Who are my people?" has gotten redefined, if not undefined, each time.

One thing I've learned is that when I say, "Hey so-and-so, I'm struggling with loneliness right now and could really use a chat with you because I love you"—as opposed to "What up, fam! Miss you! Would love to chat sometime soon!"—I almost always get a quick and tender response. I used to loath to be so obviously needy, but I'm really about that kind of assertiveness now. The inhibition-lowering and general emotional amnesty of the pandemic definitely helped.

So I cry for help more often now. And the prayers in this section have that same energy—they are my cry to God for help, and a reminder for me to be open with my friends about how much I need them.

Do you ever feel like you're almost always the more heavily invested one in friendships? We got you in this chapter. Is passive-aggressiveness a temptation for you (*Oh,* now *you can text me back? Let me take exactly as long to reply to you*)? We got you. (Where are my Enneagram 9s at, by the way?) Are you desperate for new friends but not excited about that initial banter (I blame the pandemic for my own plummeting conversation skills)? We got you.

This chapter is first in the book because, in my mind, it is the most important, and the one I most want to emphasize. If repeated, fervent prayer in this area can be a means of grace by which God makes us better friends and blesses us with better friendships, which nourishes every other area of life represented in the later chapters.

FOR SYMMETRICAL FRIENDSHIPS

O Christ, who loved us before we loved thee, and who forms us into ever more fitting objects for thy friendship, we come to thee to lament asymmetry in some of our other friendships. While we are happy to initiate, to be vulnerable, and to put in the hard work, we grow weary of doing these things unilaterally. It makes us feel unappreciated and undesired. Give us opportunity and courage to express our desires and feelings to these friends, and let us reach understanding and commitment as we set expectations for one another. Help us to love each other consistently and efficaciously, as we seek to draw one another deeper into the love of the Father, who reigns with thee and the Holy Spirit, one God, now and forever. *Amen.*

FOR WHEN ONE HAS THE OPPORTUNITY TO BE PETTY

O Christ, who whether turning tables or blowing minds was always genuine in moments of disagreement, preserve us from the perverted pleasure of pettiness. When the door is open for us to be snarky, spiteful, caustic, or passive-aggressive, help us to stroll right past it. Show us a more direct, frank, and effective way to express our hurt and frustration. And though people be tripping, let our words be dripping with the gentleness, patience, and grace of our Father, who reigns with thee and the Holy Spirit, one God, now and forever. *Amen.*

FOR WHEN ONE HAS BEEN LEFT ON READ BY A FRIEND

O Holy Spirit, who despite our frequent neglect to listen and respond doth continue to message us by revelation, inspiration, and proclamation, we come to thee having been left on read. When we feel ignored or undervalued, remind us of thine attentiveness to us. Save us from the dishonor of the double text, and help us to give the benefit of the doubt. Remind our friends of our correspondence, and put thy seal of guarantee on our resolve to be more reliable to each other in the future, for great is thy faithfulness, reigning with the Father and our Lord Jesus Christ, one God, now and forever. *Amen.*

FOR WHEN ONE IS TEMPTED TO GOSSIP

O God who brings to light all that is done in secret, we pray for thy restraining hand upon our tongues and hearts to preserve us from gossip. Keep us from the foolish justifications we invent to ease our conscience. Help us to eschew the social capital of self-bolstering sought by our flesh, and instead speak with humility and prudence, or not at all. If we must speak to a sensitive issue, help us address the concern incisively, without dishonoring others. And let us season our speech with the grace of our Lord Jesus Christ, who reigns with the Father and the Holy Spirit, one God, in glory everlasting. *Amen.*

FOR MENTORS

O Christ, whose perfect humanity inspires and empowers us daily, we give thanks for the persons in our lives whom thou hast given us to motivate and to galvanize. Let us wield any skill we have attained by thy grace to shepherd our mentees through and away from self-doubt and toward self-dedication. Make us to model industrious discipline, and use us to make the path smoother, clearer, and more direct for them than it has been for us. And may our pursuit of excellence bring us together in love and stewardship unto our Father, who reigns with thee and the Holy Spirit, one God, now and forever. *Amen.*

FOR A RELATIONSHIP QUAGMIRE

O God, who makes every effort to restore us to right relationship with thyself and with each other, we know that when we do everything we can to mend relationships, we are walking the road thou hast paved. When we have listened, repented, accepted responsibility, expressed contrition, made restitution, and requested forgiveness, help us to rest in that. If there be no improvement yet, let us not veer from our commitments, but rather continue to pray earnestly for the heart-healing which is the specialty of the Holy Spirit, who reigns with the Father and our Lord Jesus Christ, one God, in faithfulness undeterred. *Amen.*

FOR LONELINESS

O Christ, present to the masses and in fellowship with the disciples, yet understood and seen fully by none, we request thy palpable friendship for those who are lonely. When no one else is there, be our Naomi. When we feel abandoned, be our

Mary. When we are cast away, or on the run, be our Jonathan. Only thou canst bridge the deep disconnect between us. Only thou canst make us balms for each other's souls. So we ask thee to bring us true friends and an abiding love which comes from the Giver of every good gift—our Father, who reigns with thee and the Holy Spirit, one God, now and forever. *Amen.*

FOR WHEN FOLKS ARE TRYING TO JUMP ON THE BANDWAGON

O Christ, whose redemptive mission allows us all to jump on thine eschatological bandwagon, we entreat thee for patience when our friends fail to recognize our preeminent fandom, taste, and knowledge of certain cultural phenomena. Govern their thoughts, that they might realize the error of their ways and accordingly defer to us in subsequent discussions of the topics in question. And humble us, that we may not seek to be elevated or to be gatekeepers, but simply faithful administrators of cultural capital, remembering that there go we but for the grace of our Father, who reigns with thee and the Holy Spirit, one God, now and forever. *Amen.*

FOR WHEN ONE IS GETTING RAZZED BY FRIENDS

O God whose sense of humor is well-attested, preserve us when we, like Shadrach, Meshach, and Abednego, are thrown into the fire. Let this roasting not burn us but rather refine us, revealing to us how deeply we notice and amuse each other. Give us the grace and perspective to laugh at ourselves. And make this ribbing a chance to enter more deeply into relationship with one another, delighting in one another as doth our Lord Jesus Christ in us, reigning with the Father and the Holy Spirit, one God, enjoying Godself and us forever. *Amen.*

FOR WHEN ONE HAS SAID SOMETHING FOOLISH

O Spirit who knows each of our words before they leave our mouth, hear us as we lament the foolish thing(s) we have said. Though we rightly say, "Woe is me," touch the coal to our lips that our guilt may depart and our sin may be blotted out. Only thou canst tame the tongue, and cause it to yield only blessing. So help us to make reparation for our error and offense, and graciously prevent these words from haunting us. Remove the foot from our mouth and replace it with thy words of life, which are sweeter than honey, by the power of Jesus Christ the Word, who reigns with thee and our Father, one God, now and forever. *Amen.*

FOR WHEN ONE FEELS MISUNDERSTOOD

O Christ our solace, fatally misunderstood by thy friends and community, we come to thee feeling embarrassed, shamed, or misjudged. When we are not given the benefit of the doubt, remind us that thy grace sinks deep into every recess of our souls. When we feel attacked, be our hiding place, and surround us with shouts of deliverance. Rebuke and cast away the Accuser, who would love for us to get lost in a shame spiral, and instead let the voices of our friends and the Spirit call us out and sing a benediction over us, in the acceptance of the Father who lifts up our heads, who reigns with thee and the Holy Spirit, one God, in perfect understanding. *Amen.*

FOR THE AVOIDANTLY ATTACHED

O Spirit who bonds with us unbreakably in creation, covenant, redemption, and consummation, touch those who avoid attachments with others. We grieve the neglect and dismissal that led to this mechanism of survival. Steadily demonstrate to us that we do not have to regulate our emotions entirely on our own. Bring to us true friends who dependably seek to attune and respond to us, and nudge us if we begin to avoid them. Show us the beauty of interdependence, and reconnect us to the desire, memory, and emotion, which comprise the abundant life of our Lord Jesus Christ, who reigns with thee and our Father, one God, in perfect unity. *Amen.*

FOR A ROAD TRIP

O God who goes behind, beside, and before us on the road to glory, we ask thy blessing upon this road trip. Kindly make our navigation expeditious, our views bucolic, our conversation delightful, and our snacks delectable. Inspire the mind of the one to whom thou wilt entrust the power of the aux cord, that they might put together a playlist which slaps. Preserve us from road rage when fellow drivers are acting a fool. And protect us from accidents and all other dangers, by the travel mercies of our Lord Jesus Christ, who reigns with our Father and the Holy Spirit, one God, forever and ever. *Amen.*

FOR GOODBYES

O Christ, whose farewell came with the promise of the Spirit and of thy triumphant return, help us to say goodbye well. Give us fortitude to lean into the sadness and loss, and the words to express what we have meant to one another. When possible, give us the means and the commitment to stay in touch. Console us if one or both parties fail to do so. Help us to savor the moments we have with those in our lives now, knowing how quickly things can change. And bring us to that day of joyful and unending reunions in the consummated community of our Father, who reigns with thee and the Holy Spirit, one God, world without end. *Amen.*

FOR ONE'S SQUAD

O God of David and Jonathan, we are grateful for our close friends. With every check-in text, every nickname coined, every frustration vented, every hurt comforted, and every love language spoken, they have been thine instruments, helping us to image our relational, triune God. Help us to soak up every probing conversation, every comfortable silence, and every knowing glance. Use us to bless and delight them. Bind us together with a covenant to show we love each other as our own souls, and seal it with the guarantee of the Holy Spirit, who reigns with the Father and our Lord Jesus Christ, one God, in friendship everlasting. *Amen.*

FOR BEFORE THIRD-WHEELING

O God in whom three is the perfect interpersonal number, be with us when we find ourselves to be the third wheel. We ascribe to thee the good vibes of couples who have mastered the art of being with others without making them feel awkward, excluded, or lonely, and we ask thee to do a similar work in other couples. Allow us to develop our individual relationship with each of them in addition to relating to them jointly, and help us to bless each other out of the unique richness of our different vocations of singleness or partnership, given to each by the Holy Spirit, who reigns with our Father and our Lord Jesus Christ, one God, now and forever. *Amen.*

FOR INVITING OTHERS INTO ONE'S STRUGGLE

O Christ our companion in the way, help us to ascertain how and whom to invite into the inner circle amongst whom we share the defining struggles of our lives. Reveal to us who has shown themselves to be a secure place for our insecurities, a soft shoulder to cry on, and a cheerleader for every victory, big and small. Help us to communicate our needs well. Give them a love for us which seeks understanding, yet listens and laments even when it cannot find it. And carry them as they carry our burdens, Jesus our strength, who reigns with our Father and the Holy Spirit, one God, now and forever. *Amen.*

FOR GOOD COMMUNICATION IN RELATIONSHIPS

O Spirit who reveals thy will to us, we entreat thy governance over our communication with loved ones. Teach us their love languages, and help us understand their motivations and perspectives, that we might not talk past each other but rather directly to the heart. Keep us from expecting them to read our minds, or to abide by unspoken rules, but rather let us frankly and respectfully express what we want, need, and expect. And make us willing and happy to adjust out of love for them, as doth our Lord Jesus Christ in accommodating to us, who reigns with thee and our Father, one God, in perfect understanding. *Amen.*

FOR BEFORE A REBUKE

O Christ, who rebuked thy disciples and family for the sake of love, show us how to admonish and correct righteously. Govern our emotions, that our needful rebuke might reject a spirit of pride and bitterness for one of lament. When pushback is righteous and well informed, help us receive it. If third-party counsel is needed, show us to it. Shepherd us through the emotional toll of broken communion, and finally deliver us unto the justice which enables the reconciliation administered by the Holy Spirit, who reigns with thee and our Father, one God, now and forever. *Amen.*

FOR THOSE WHOSE LOVE LANGUAGE IS PHYSICAL TOUCH

O God who holds us, carries us, and imparts life through thy touch, receive into thine arms those who love to be loved through physical affection. Help us to offset the touch deprivation of our culture. Do make us sensitive to those who have had bad experience with touch, and to those who are simply inclined differently. Yet do kindly make a way for hugs, cuddles, kisses, and other demonstrations which release oxytocin, dopamine, and serotonin, raising our spirits as we draw each other ever more into the embrace of Father, Son, and Holy Spirit, one God, world without end. *Amen.*

FOR WHEN ONE NEEDS TO APOLOGIZE

O Spirit who repairs those who repent, when we have sinned against another, prompt us to ask for forgiveness. Make our heart uneasy and our mind unsettled, yet teach us to distinguish thy convicting work from the shame which seeks to masquerade in thy place, for only the former provides grace and power to be made whole and to make right. During and following our apology, make our contrition clear, our recompense concrete, and our life amended, and reap the fruit of obedience within us and between us: the peace of our Lord Jesus Christ, who reigns with thee and our Mother, one God, now and forever. *Amen.*

FOR WHEN ONE NEEDS TO FORGIVE

O Father without whose forgiveness we have no hope, help us extend mercy to those who have wronged us. We give up any and all perceived right to exact judgment or retribution, for thou hast commanded us to enjoy the blessing of leaving these to thee. If true apology and reparation have been offered, show us if reconciliation is possible, and if so, how to pursue it healthfully. And keep our tongues from the poisons of bitterness and pride; instead, make us drink deeply of the wisdom which can salvage love out of the wreckage of sins committed against us, by the power of the Holy Spirit, who reigns with thee and our Lord Jesus Christ, one God, now and forever. *Amen.*

FOR LETTING GO OF TOXIC RELATIONSHIPS

O Mother who holds us fast, open our hands to let go of toxic relationships. Shake the dust off our feet as we move on. In every place that's been obscured, distorted, or gaslit, shine thy clarifying light, and for every loss on the investment of our selves, recoup relational wisdom for our future. Evict these relationships from their occupation of our inner lives, and usher in positive experiences to supersede the former, through Christ who heals our hearts, who reigns with thee and the Holy Spirit, one God, restoring all things. *Amen.*

FOR WHEN ONE HAS BEEN LEFT OUT

O Christ, who was excluded that we might be included, rejected that we might be accepted, and passed over that we might be sought out, soften the sting and dull the pain of being left out. Bring us to new doors that we might not merely look into but enter fully, and to tables thou hast set for us. While we wait to be seen, draw us ever more into thy love, which was not and will not be deterred in choosing us through the call of the Holy Spirit, who reigns with thee and our Father, one God, now and forever. *Amen.*

FOR WHEN ONE MUST MAKE SMALL TALK

O Christ, who spoke the world into existence and later spoke to us as one of us, we commend ourselves to thee as we prepare to make small talk. Though it seem mundane or inconsequential, make it a way to show hospitality to those we know not well. Though it feel disingenuous, make it a portal to deeper connection. When we know not what to say, give us the perfectly innocuous words by which we might put others at ease and make them feel seen, as thou dost for our souls in the mundane moments of the abundant life given and sustained by our Lord Jesus Christ, who reigns with the Father and the Holy Spirit, one God, world without end. *Amen.*

II

SINGLENESS
AND ROMANCE

AS I NOTED in the Introduction, this is the area of life that gave rise to this entire project. It's also the space that felt most underrepresented, not just in the formal prayer tradition but in the spiritual formation resources of the church as a whole. We were not taught healthy (or really any) dating ethics or practices in my youth group. The implicit messaging was something like "Remain pure, walk with the Lord, and God will reveal to you who God has ordained for you to marry. Once that happens, you'll go immediately into serious courting mode, and then premarital counseling, and on to marriage within a year—year and a half at the latest."

Many of us who grew up in purity culture have done (and are still doing) the hard work of deconstructing it. But it's hard to reconstruct something different and better when there aren't many devotional resources to help us do so. The prayers in this chapter, which made up the majority of the first thirty or so collects that I wrote for this project, helped me begin to organize my values and perspective on healthy dating practices.

Being a serial crusher with a never-stay-down approach to dating has its funny moments, its déjà vu moments, its epiphany moments, and its deeply despairing moments. I needed prayers for all of them. I needed to articulate the sanctification opportunity that I've found to always be present within the process of asking someone out. I needed to crystallize the courage, the vulnerability, the wordsmithing, the waiting, and the anticipation into a set form that I could go back to when I inevitably found myself there again. I needed a record of the spiritual workout that I was doing, so that I could share my regimen with others and maybe add ten more pounds on the next rep.

The collect "for single folk who have a deep desire for marriage and children" was requested by an admired acquaintance of mine who blessedly became a friend through my writing of the prayer. It was precious to see the response online from folks who, like this friend, were long past the age where they had expected or hoped to be married with kids, and had carried that low-grade sadness for years, and were now feeling seen and interceded for in that particular space for perhaps the first time, or at least the first time in the form of a public call to prayer.

And that's what these collects are—not only prayers, but also reminders and calls to pray for particular people and concerns. I pray that this book functions not only as "I just had this experience—I wonder if there's a prayer in here for this," but also as "Wow, you know, I did not realize that I should be praying for this, but of course I should, and here are some words to get me started."

FOR WHEN ONE IS ENAMORED
BUT MUST BE CHILL ABOUT IT

O Unmoved Mover, whose burden is easy and whose yoke is light, we beseech thee now for the chill which so easily eludes us. By the still, small voice of thy Spirit, make us still. By the steadiness of thy hand, calm our restless hearts. By the steadfastness of thy love, make us patient in all manner of romantic captivation, for the right ordering of love toward others which is the mark of the kingdom of our Lord Jesus Christ, who reigns with thee and the Holy Spirit, one God, now and forever. *Amen.*

FOR BEFORE SHOOTING ONE'S SHOT

O Christ, who boldly went out of thy way to see, affirm, and connect with Zacchaeus, the woman at the well, and many others, we entreat thee for courage as we prepare to shoot our shot. We pause to recognize that this person is thine exquisite and beloved creation, with dignity and fullness of life beyond that which we can know now. Fill us with the Spirit, the breath of God, before we take this plunge. Make us articulate, forthright, and winsome, that they might see in us potential for a connection that might be fulfilling to them and glorifying to our Father, who reigns with thee and the Holy Spirit, one God, in love everlasting. *Amen.*

FOR AFTER SHOOTING ONE'S SHOT

O Christ, who offered thyself up to the greatest vulnerability of all—we have put ourselves out there, and we beseech thee to be with us out here. In the anticipation, the wondering, the fear, the self-doubt, the exposure, be our anchor, our tether, our gravitational center. Govern the deliberations of this cutie, that whatever they think or feel, they may be kind, respectful, and expeditious in their response. We ascribe to thee the courage it has taken to arrive thus far, and we ask a double portion of it as we wait in the power of the one who always sees us and desires us, thou who reigns with the Father and the Holy Spirit, one God, now and forever. *Amen.*

FOR AFTER BEING TURNED DOWN

O Lord of empathy, well acquainted with all of our sorrows and the sting of unfulfilled hope, we seek to rest our weary heads and hearts in thy loving embrace. We ask for thy consolation as we feel rejected, unseen, or unloved. We do thank thee for the opportunity to be emotionally courageous. We thank thee for the ways in which thou hast and wilt use this to form us into Christ's likeness. We thank thee for fashioning us with a desire to love deeply, and we ask that this desire would meet its right end in the perfect timing of our Lord Jesus Christ, who reigns with thee and the Holy Spirit, one God, now and forever. *Amen.*

FOR WHEN THEY'RE PICKING UP
WHAT YOU'RE LAYING DOWN

O Christ, who daily shows us more of thy love and of our belovedness, we rejoice in thee that we seem to be vibing with the person we are seeing. Thou hast brought to us one who gets us, reminding us of the way thou knowest us better than we know ourselves. One who sees us as special, reminding us of thy personal delight in us. We lift our hearts in excitement, and open our hands to hold this relationship up to thy providence. So kindly light one step of the path at a time, and if it be thy will, let us walk it together a long way, helping each other to follow after our Father, who reigns with thee and the Holy Spirit, one God, world without end. *Amen.*

FOR LETTING SOMEONE DOWN EASY

O gentle Father, whose "no" cometh always in perfect compassion, we ask thee to fill us with empathy as we prepare to let down one of thy beloved children. Grateful for the time we've shared, we give thanks for them. Well acquainted with such disappointment, we do this only with humility and heaviness in our hearts. Aware of their vulnerability, we wield our power mindfully and lovingly. Make our words soft, their hearts resilient, our communication clear, and their recovery quick, by the consolation of the Holy Spirit, who reigns with thee and our Lord Jesus Christ, one God, now and forever. *Amen.*

FOR BIPOC WITH WHITE PARTNERS

O Christ, disparate from yet walking with us, we commend to thee all non-white folk who have white partners. Make these relationships never hinder but rather only foster investment in their own culture and identity. Lead them, through the hard work of conveying and entrusting the deepest parts of themselves, to form virtue which overflows into all their friendships. Give their partners the discipline and resourcefulness with which to grow every day in their cultural competency and solidarity, having their love made more comprehensive by the expansive work of the Holy Spirit, who reigns with thee and our Father, one God, now and forever. *Amen.*

FOR AN INTERNET CRUSH

O Spirit for whom our love, by thy providence, is always sensible and practical, guide our discernment with regard to the online cutie in whom we have become interested. As thou hast governed the intersection of our Web surfing, do the same for our sliding into each other's DMs. If geographic proximity be lacking, show us whether other forms of compatibility might nevertheless be strong enough to warrant further exploration. And give us a lasting friend or even partner who both on- and offline deepens our love for our Lord Jesus Christ, who reigns with thee and our Father, one God, now and forever. *Amen.*

FOR WHEN YOU WANT TO BE THEIR LOVER AND THEREFORE HAVE TO GET WITH THEIR FRIENDS

O Father who befriends us individually and collectively, strengthen our bonds with the friends of our beloved. Give them to us as other sources of input, celebration, and accountability for our relationships, that we might receive their blessings and learn from them how to best love our partner. Yet also give them to us as friends in our own right, that we might have our own unique connections, dynamics, and inside jokes with each other. And let wisdom flow into and out of our relationships from and into our wider communities by the unitive ministry of the Holy Spirit, who reigns with thee and our Lord Jesus Christ, one God, now and forever. *Amen.*

FOR A NEW RELATIONSHIP

O Christ, with whom our love is daily renewed, we ascribe to thee benevolence and sovereignty over this new relationship. At thy throne we lay down our fear of mistakes and missteps, our uncertainty about how we are being perceived, and our ongoing vulnerability, and we take up thy yoke which is easy. Help us to hear, through the combination of our instincts, our learned wisdom, our communication with our partner, and our prayers, thy will for how we are to proceed. And do amplify the wonder and excitement of this time by the upswell of the Holy Spirit, who reigns with thee and our Father, one God, in glory everlasting. *Amen.*

FOR LONG-DISTANCE RELATIONSHIPS

O Holy Spirit, lofty and inaccessible in many ways yet also unbelievably near to us, we pray for those in long-distance relationships. We thank thee for the technology which makes them easier, but we lament the many ways in which they are difficult, not least the lack of touch, the travel, and the gaps in rhythms of people and place. Thou art able to work through these unique and challenging growing conditions—use this period to nurture us, yet do graciously and expeditiously bring it to an end, aligning our trajectories by the providence of our Father, who reigns with thee and our Lord Jesus Christ, one God, now and forever. *Amen.*

FOR BEFORE MEETING ONE'S PARTNER'S FAMILY

O Spirit who goes before us in all our interactions, prepare us to meet the family of our beloved. Make our love for our partner evident, and our devotion undeniable. Where their relationships with family are rocky, make us attentive and show us the best way to support. Where they are rich, show us how to treasure and protect them. Lead us to a deeper knowledge of our partner through relationship with those who have shaped them. And if possible, give us the family's blessing, and make our dreams for our beloved coincide, by the providence of our Lord Jesus Christ, who reigns with thee and our Father, one God, now and forever. *Amen.*

FOR WHEN ONE HAS ACCIDENTALLY LIKED THEIR CRUSH'S OLD PHOTO

O Spirit who hovered over the waters at creation, and hovers over us now with careful grace, unlike our fingers over this photo of our crush, help us. Though we often pray against technical difficulties, in this case we do entreat thee to confound the operations of [social media platform], that the notification might be cast away as far as the east is from the west. And if this be thy providential voice telling us to renounce our stalking and instead gird ourselves to shoot our shot, let us heed the leading of our Lord Jesus Christ, who reigns with thee and our Father, one God, now and forever. *Amen.*

FOR A DTR

O Spirit who sheds thy clarifying light upon all obscurity, we entreat thee to govern our impending attempts to clear up relationships which suffer from imprecise definition or vague expectation. Let our commitment to love win out over our fear of rejection. Let our devotion to candor and kindness soften the impact of words which are hard to speak or hear. If possible, let our talk reveal us to already be of one accord, yet if not, let it reveal exactly what we hope to be to each other going forward, in the mutual understanding made possible by the unitive ministry of our Lord Jesus Christ, who reigns with thee and the Father, one God, now and forever. *Amen.*

FOR GOING TO A WEDDING WHILE SINGLE

O True Lover, well acquainted with loneliness, we come to thee as we enter a space that turns the dull pain of loneliness into a sharp twinge. As much as we seek to celebrate what thou hast done in the lives of our friends, we cannot help but feel the absence of similar divine provision in our own. Do supplement our strength to rejoice with those who rejoice, and do meet us in the moments of our sadness, and do give us hope in thy future provision. May we be used now to lift spirits as thy Son didst when he fashioned and provided the best wine at

Cana—Jesus Christ, who reigns with thee and the Holy Spirit, one God, now and forever. *Amen.*

FOR WHEN ONE NEEDS TO BE BLINDED TO SOMEONE'S HOTNESS

O Father, sovereign over all our affect, thou hast made it clear that a relationship with a certain cutie is not thy will for us, yet the attraction regrettably does not yet subside. We do praise thee for this person's beauty, but we ask that our visceral response to it be either dulled or transformed into some more temperate or neutral disposition, in order to produce the most appropriate interactions for the building up of the kingdom of our Lord Jesus Christ, who reigns with thee and the Holy Spirit, one God, world without end. *Amen.*

FOR SINGLE FOLK SEEING HAPPY COUPLE PHOTOS ON SOCIAL MEDIA

O Jesus Christ, High Priest who sympathizes with us in all our weakness, we come to thee as our scrolling has sparked or amplified feelings of loneliness, sadness, or unluckiness. Preserve us from bitterness and envy. Uplift us to rejoice with those who rejoice, yet meet us in these moments of our sadness, and do give us hope in thy future provision. And graciously cleanse our palate by way of humorous meme or cute cat video, as thou dost cleanse our souls daily with the hyssop of the Father, who reigns with thee and the Holy Spirit, one God, now and forever. *Amen.*

FOR BEFORE OPENING A DATING APP

O Lord of each and every age, leaven of each generation, we ask thee to work through this app as thou hast worked through all manner of dating practices across time and space. Help us to remember that each face we see here is not merely a profile, but a person. Not a product to be consumed or rejected, but a beautiful creation, with a life, a story, and a desire to be known and loved. Guide our interactions so as to be forthright, respectful, and dignifying to the other. Protect our heart as we make ourselves vulnerable and entrust the results to thee, as did our Lord Jesus Christ, who reigns with thee and the Holy Spirit, one God, now and forever. *Amen.*

FOR AFTER GETTING GHOSTED

O Holy Ghost, we come to thee having been ghosted in most unholy fashion. Unchanging, ever-present Lord, we seek refuge in thee as we wonder whence this change and whence this sudden absence. We lament the indifference with which we have been treated, the accountability which is lacking, and the fair expectations which were broken. We seek not to ascribe motives or pronounce judgment, but we do ask that wrongs be redressed. Preserve us from questioning ourselves and what we could have done differently. We ask that thou, O comforting Father, would heal our hearts and our culture, and restore to us the joy of our Lord Jesus Christ, who reigns with thee and the Holy Spirit, one God, now and forever. *Amen.*

FOR WEIGHING A RELATIONSHIP

O Spirit of calculated love, who gives us wants, needs, experiences, and ideals as tools for faithful discernment, order our thoughts. Help us identify the strengths and weaknesses of our relationship as they are, and count the cost of staying as well as leaving. Distinguish healthy expectations from unproductive ones. Reveal what of our ideals we can afford to deny or defer, and which are essential for the creation and sustenance of the desire which can become a school for virtue. Make us both objectively and subjectively deft, after the wisdom of our Lord Jesus Christ, who reigns with thee and our Father, one God, now and forever. *Amen.*

FOR AFTER GETTING DUMPED

O Man of Sorrows, betrayed by those you loved so fervently, let down by those who declared they would never fail you—be near to those of us whose relationship has ended. Speak to us in the sheer sound of silence. Be with us in the stark feeling of loneliness. Rebuke the Accuser who would seek now to convince us of lies. Illuminate us and govern our thoughts as we seek to process what happened. Place your scarred hands upon our wounded heart, and lead us down the path of healing. Harvest the good from this relationship; plant it deep in the ground of our soul, and bring forth life from this death, O God our Cultivator, through Jesus the true Vine, in the resurrection power of the Holy Spirit, one God, now and forever. *Amen.*

FOR WHEN ONE HAS THE OPPORTUNITY TO REBOUND

O Christ, who bounced back from death and the grave, show us, when love drops us, to seek no other landing place but thee. When we feel the emptiness of a newly opened void, help us adjust to it, and not attempt in haste to fill it with something or someone else. If potential loves come to mind, make us mind thy work of healing in us, that we might defer our desire for them rather than treat them as deferred prospects for love. Yet do bring us friends who affirm our worth and winsomeness through the kindness of the Holy Spirit, who reigns with thee and our Mother, one God, world without end. *Amen.*

FOR WHEN ONE DESIRES TO BE SET UP

O Treasurer of our undisclosed desires, well acquainted with our readiness to give and receive romantic love, we thank thee for all the wonderful companions thou hast given us, as well as for all of their friends whom we do not know. Do help our friends to see our desire and to demonstrate love to us in the form of setting us up with one of the latter (perhaps especially [name]). Open their eyes to see which connection(s) would be fire, and their hearts to feel the big rom-com energy that could proceed from their actions. We do believe that this is one of the best ways to meet folks, and so we hope this request aligns with the will of our Lord Jesus Christ, who reigns with thee and the Holy Spirit, one God, now and forever. *Amen.*

FOR GOING ON A SETUP

O Knower of all that is unknown to us, certain in our uncertainty and sovereign over our romantic risks, we rest in the fact that thou knowest both parties intimately and hast in thy providence arranged for our paths to cross. We give thanks to thee for the mutual friend(s) which have seen beauty in us individually, and potentially in us together. We implore thee for connection, clarity, and openness in our conversation, as well as for the balance of levity and gravity with which thou so lovingly governeth us—thou our Lord Jesus Christ, who reigns with the Father and the Holy Spirit, one God, now and forever. *Amen.*

FOR WHEN ONE IS UNSURE AFTER ONE OR A FEW DATES

O Spirit who makes us self-aware, deciphering the messages of gut, heart, and mind, aid our discernment when we are unsure whether or not to continue seeing someone. Teach us what weight to place on each aspect of perceived compatibility, and a sense for how to give it enough time without wasting anyone's time. Give us a nudge in one direction, and the ability to follow through in a way that dignifies both parties and holds gently the ambiguity present in any romantic choice we make with the help of our Father, who reigns with thee and our Lord Jesus Christ, one God, now and forever. *Amen.*

FOR WHEN FRIENDS GET ENGAGED

O Christ our Bridegroom, we come to thee rejoicing in the betrothal of our loved ones. Thou art the author of love, and of their love in particular, and for this we give thee praise. Kindly make this period of engagement for them a bountiful time of joy and fulfillment; of loving and knowing, and of being loved and known ever more deeply. Through experience and counsel prepare them for this new life. When conflicts arise, give them the humility and wisdom to resolve them. Unite their families. Make us a bulwark and a buoy for them. And as they plan their wedding, draw them into the joy of our great wedding to the Lamb, who unites us to the Father, who reigns with thee and the Holy Spirit, one God, now and forever. *Amen.*

FOR WHEN YOU'RE WAITING FOR THEM TO BE THE ONE YOU'RE WAITING FOR

O Spirit of patient love, teach us poise and grit in our yearning. When all we can do is wait, make our affection deeply potent in its dormancy, like magma underneath the surface. When hope is real yet deferred, let our love be like coal with diamond dreams. When reciprocation is scarce, help us to put our love in low-power mode. And make this time a chrysalis of our patient transformation by our Lord Jesus Christ, who reigns with thee and our Father, one God, now and forever. *Amen.*

FOR WHEN LOVE FEELS HOPELESSLY ELUSIVE

O God who sees, knows, desires, and pursues us, come within our reach when love continues to elude our grasp. Be our soft landing place when our flight ends in yet another crash, or when we fail to get off the ground at all. When desire is met with undesirability, vulnerability with rejection, sustained effort with a moving target, hope with disappointment, and self-disclosure with inscrutability, meet us in our despair with a love that dignifies us. And as long as our desire is unfulfilled, make the desire itself a generator of the fruit of the Holy Spirit, who reigns with thee and our Lord Jesus Christ, one God, now and forever. *Amen.*

FOR THE LOVE THAT HAS BEEN ELUSIVE

O Source of every good gift, of whom we ask with hopeful yet unentitled expectation, bring us the love we long for. A love which can be a vehicle for thy redemption of the rejection and loneliness we have experienced. A love which demonstrates our desirability over against the ways we've been treated as undesirable. A love which allows us to sow where we reap. A love which banks on us. A love which is conceived in hope, developed in trust, and consummated in the faithfulness shown to us by our Lover Jesus Christ, who reigns with thee and the Holy Spirit, one God, now and forever. *Amen.*

FOR SINGLE FOLK WHO HAVE A DEEP DESIRE FOR MARRIAGE AND CHILDREN

O Father, defender of our dreams, safeguard of our unfulfilled desires, we lift up to thee single folk who continue to long deeply for marriage and children. We lament the ends of relationships that seemed promising, the feeling of being invisible or undesirable, the loneliness, and the inability to live and love in ways we are sure we were created for. At thy throne of grace we are bold to ask for full and timely provision of a spouse and little ones. In thy bosom of consolation we wait in faith. As we do so, make thy will increasingly clear, and bring us into other relationships where the love we receive and give surprises us by its depth and longevity, becoming a faithful foretaste of the love which subsumes all loves—that of the Father, Son, and Holy Spirit, one God, now and forever. *Amen.*

III

FAMILY
AND HOME

YOU KNOW HOW Netflix has vastly expanded our collective sense of how many different kinds or categories of TV show there are? I'm looking at the algorithm's mind control—I mean, suggestions—on my home page right now: offbeat comedies, irreverent showbiz comedies, cerebral dramas, lovable losers, bingeworthy, watch in one weekend, suburban dysfunction, and so on.

My favorite of their descriptors is "chosen family." A big part of the evergreen appeal of big hits like *The Office, Parks and Recreation, New Girl, 30 Rock,* etc., is the way in which a bunch of ragtag misfits commit to being not just "workplace proximity associates" or roommates or friends of friends, but people who are inextricably, irremovably interwoven into one another's lives on a daily basis. They go out of their way to create a home out of their shared space. They turn down opportunities in order to stay with one another. They create common rituals and rhythms. They fight. They communicate. They develop together as characters. At a certain point, they become so intertwined that they couldn't fully get away from one another even if they wanted to.

For me, that's family crystallized. Whether bonded by blood and marriage or by soul and spirit (or both), who are the people whose love isn't going anywhere? With whom can I find the *hesed,* the covenant faithfulness of Ruth and Naomi?

Who will be the one to say to me, "Where you go I will go, your God will be my God, your people will be my people, even when our worldviews diverge, even when I have to draw boundaries, even when you feel like I can never fully enter into this or that part of your life, even when you seem incapable of seeing things the way I see them, even when we hurt each other, even when you rebuke me for what I've done or failed to do."

In the Introduction, I hinted at the idea that formal prayer is like infrastructure that houses, supports, directs, and shapes our extemporaneous devotion. Whatever I have to say from the creativity of my own heart is only grounded and amplified by what I am encouraged to say with the carefully crafted and balanced words of the prayer book.

I think of family analogously. It's the covenantal commitment, the set of practices and ethics for aligning multiple infinitely unique people, the rule of life that in turn creates the consistent space for "extemporaneous" interactions.

I was talking recently with a good friend who's been married for about a year. I told him that I desperately wanted more relationships that were "built-in," in which I didn't have to set up hangouts every time because there's a regular, expected routine of being together. He, on the other hand, lamented that after a year of marriage (with half of that being stay-at-home due to the pandemic), he and his wife were sorely lacking in intentional "date" time, despite having tons of "built-in presence" time.

It's very easy from my vantage point to see his grass as greener, and maybe it truly is, but in either case the conversation reminded me that as a single guy intentionally reaching out, I'm building muscles that I'll need (God willing) in marriage, and that married people can conversely offer some of the built-in presence of their lives to single folk. Wherever you find yourself on that relational spectrum, I pray that there are collects in here for your circumstance.

FOR THOSE ABOUT TO BE GRILLED BY RELATIVES

O long-suffering Christ, who reminded thy holy mother that thy time had not yet come, we entreat thee for patience as we prepare to be with our relatives and be grilled like so much fish from the Sea of Galilee. We thank thee for their attentiveness, but we ask thee to help them to prioritize love for who we are now over their expectations of who we could be. Assist us in whatever combination of deflection, distraction, abstraction, or prepared statement may prove necessary. And do redirect these conversations toward less trying topics, as thou dost redirect us out of all folly to the wisdom of the Father, who guides us along with thee and the Holy Spirit, one God, now and forever. *Amen.*

FOR BEREAVED MOTHERS

O Christ, whose mother our queen plumbed the depths of grief upon thy death, we beseech thee to hold fast all mothers whose children have died. Take their hand and lead them through this stark perversion, this visceral guttedness, this loss of their delight, their heart, their world. Bring them to others who know their pain, and make them their support as they seek justice, solace, or strength. Preserve their lives and the souls of their children, that they might be reunited in thine unending triumph, the death of death, the consummated world of our Mother who reigns with thee and the Holy Spirit, one God, in glory everlasting. *Amen.*

FOR PETS

O Father who rescued us and made us an indispensable part of thy family, we commend to thee our pets. Endearing them to us, thou hast expanded our capacity for love. By their estimation of us thou hast illustrated thine unmerited favor. So, with every caretaking responsibility discharged, and with every expense paid, teach us a commensurate devotion. And as we manage our pets' Instagram accounts, remind us of thy surpassing pride in us and proclamation thereof by the mighty voice of the Holy Spirit, who reigns with thee and our Lord Jesus Christ, one God, now and forever. *Amen.*

FOR BEFORE TAKING A SHOWER

O Spirit who cleanses us thoroughly from all our iniquities, wash us now. Make this soap, like thy grace, cover us from head to toe, finding every nook and cranny. Make the stream strong and hot to massage sore muscles. Clear our minds and bring us into a state of meditation, that we might receive shower epiphanies. Condition us, making us ever softer and healthier in spirit. And as we belt out melodies, make our cry a shout of triumph unto our Father, who reigns with thee and our Lord Jesus Christ, one God, in glory everlasting. *Amen.*

FOR THOSE STRUGGLING TO CONCEIVE

O God of Sarah, Hannah, and Elizabeth, by whose touch life blossoms in unexpected ways, we implore thee to succor those struggling to conceive. Whether through traditional or more novel means, may it be thy will to bless them with pregnancy and healthy delivery. If thy will be different, kindly reveal this, and console them, and show them where and how to direct their call to nurture. Ease the aches of longing which arise at the sight of other families with children. Preserve them in hope, and shape them through this yearning by thy sanctifying Holy Spirit, who lives and reigns with thee and our Lord Jesus Christ in glory everlasting. *Amen.*

FOR A PREGNANCY

O incarnate Christ, who graced the womb of our holy mother and knits us together in utero, we commend these expectant parents unto thee. As with thy creation of the world, orchestrate the development of this child in overflowing possibility and mysterious beauty. Kindly ease the illness, aches, and other travails of the childbearer, as much as possible. Make their partner a source of constant support and reassurance. Preserve this child through these months, through a healthy delivery, and on to an abundant life. And prepare these to be loving and wise parents through the example of our Father, who nurtures us along with thee and the Holy Spirit, one God, now and forever. *Amen.*

FOR AFTER A MISCARRIAGE

O Christ, who wept upon the death of thy beloved, we lift up to thee childbearers whose pregnancies have been lost. Filled with expectation and now emptied by sadness, stabilize and restore their souls. Overwhelmed by first the mysterious gift and now the inscrutable loss, show them how to grieve in a world of senseless pain and futility. Show thyself to be the redeemer of all snatched hopes and false starts. Give them the inexplicable strength to move forward, and in thy timing allow them to fulfill the call to parenthood given to them by our Father, who reigns with thee and the Holy Spirit, one God, in glory everlasting. *Amen.*

FOR WHEN ONE CLOGS THE TOILET

O Spirit who clears away all that which obstructs us from thy grace, we beseech thy deliverance—both from the backup we have unwittingly caused, and from the concomitant embarrassment. Make our plunging effective, or our recourse quick to those with more plumbing expertise. Send forth air fresheners whose pleasing aromas arise like the prayers of the saints. And let the waters flow pure and clean once again, as at Horeb didst our Father, who reigns with thee and our Lord Jesus Christ, one God, now and forever. *Amen.*

FOR WHEN ONE SEES A PEST IN THE HOUSE

O Father who exterminates all evil, as thou hast shorn our feet with the gospel of peace, so also make them fleet to avoid cockroaches, mice, and other unwelcome cohabitants. Make our eyes sharp and our hands quick to catch and release, that we might remove them humanely. Illuminate and uncover the obscured recesses of this space, as thou hast done to the parts of our lives where sin resides. Bring these creatures to a new and better home, and help us to foster rather than destroy such habitats, as our Lord Jesus Christ hast done for us, reigning with thee and the Holy Spirit, one God, in glory everlasting. *Amen.*

FOR SAYING GOODBYE TO A PLACE

O God in whom we are planted, we praise thee for bringing us to and setting down our roots in this place. Help us now to say goodbye in a way that soothes our souls; amplify memories, illuminate the evidences of thy faithful providence, and give us closure. As we retrace study nooks, playing fields, eateries, places of fellowship, and sacred spaces, imprint on our minds images which we can keep with us. Send with us that which made our house a home. And let this bittersweetness remind us how we have tasted and seen that the Lord is good, who reigns—Father, Son, and Holy Spirit, now and forever. *Amen.*

FOR THOSE WHO GIVE FOSTER CARE

O Father in whom all may find security and belonging, we lift up to thee those who give foster care. For their dedication of financial, emotional, and relational resources to this vocation, bless them. Through bureaucracy and red tape, advance them. To be reliable fountains of nurture, empower them. In the bittersweet moments when kids move on to other homes, console them. To whichever relationship with biological families may be best, lead them. And may all members of these homes go from strength to strength by the care of he who fosters all our development, our Lord Jesus Christ, who reigns with thee and the Holy Spirit, one God, in perfect love. *Amen.*

FOR ROOMMATES

O Christ, who chose to make thine itinerant home with twelve friends, we pray for those with whom we share domesticity. Though we may have come together out of necessity, let us grow together in mutual care and interwoven rhythms. Whether by rule of life or other arrangement, help us to set expectations and disciplines for our collective practices, both mundane and special. Help us to address conflict swiftly and respectfully. And as we come home to each other daily, help us bring each other home to our Father, who reigns with thee and the Holy Spirit, one God, now and forever. *Amen.*

FOR WHEN THE CAR IS ACTING UP

O Spirit who transports us to the throne room of God, we ask thy preservation over our vehicle. Protect us from all dangers attended by its dysfunction. Give our mechanic perception and wisdom, and bless them for their work. Save us from costly repairs, yet give us means to fix what is wrong. And for those of us whose car is itself old enough to drive, please give us means to purchase a new one soon, or bring us to a place with public transit, that we might be safe and economical as we live and move and have our being in thee, who reigns with the Father and our Lord Jesus Christ, one God, now and forever. *Amen.*

FOR WHEN ONE'S VIEWS DRIFT
FROM THOSE OF ONE'S PARENTS'

O Christ, whose parents loved thee but at times failed to understand thine identity and mission, we ask thy preservation over our relationships with our parental figures. When we strike out on our own, as thou didst into the temple and later into the world, may we remain connected to where we come from, and sensitive to the fact that our parents do not share the same experiences. When our changing perspectives clash, may we seek to continue to move toward one another, if possible, and have healthy discussion. If rupture be inevitable, may it be respectful, and restore us to each other in the future, as thou dost restore all things, reigning with the Father and the Holy Spirit, one God, now and forever. *Amen.*

FOR A TRANSRACIAL ADOPTION

O Christ, brought up in a family which was providentially apt, and yet vastly disparate from thee, we ask thy governance over all seeking to adopt transracially. Kindly bless these hopeful parents for this desire and commitment. Commit them to growth in cultural humility and competency, that this child may have ample opportunity to invest in and be shaped by their multiple heritages. Facilitate this adoption process, and give this child the robust sense of self which comes by being known expansively, and loved deeply, as shown to us by our Father, who reigns with thee and the Holy Spirit, one God, in bond unbreakable. *Amen.*

FOR WHEN GROCERIES ARE LOW
BUT ONE HAS TO MAKE SOMETHING

O God who does much with little, who made the flour and oil runneth over for the widow of Zarephath, we ask thy assistance as we seek to make something to eat from what is left in the fridge and cupboards. Give us creativity to imagine alternative combinations, contentment with simple recipes, and sustenance with the little we have left on hand. In so doing, remind us of the breadth of what thou hast done with the little we offer unto our Lord Jesus Christ, who reigns with thee and the Holy Spirit, one God, now and forever. *Amen.*

FOR NEWLYWEDS

O God of new beginnings, guarantor of covenants—we entreat thee to advance thy work of building this new family, home, and life together. Let the wedding jubilance now give way to small, everyday celebrations of love. Establish new traditions and rhythms. Let their devotion overflow to their friends and neighbors. Form in them an open, sacrificial heart with which to tackle transitions and challenges. And enable them to weave their lives together, as thou didst with us through thine incarnation and continue to do through thy Spirit, in the love of the Father, one God, world without end. *Amen.*

FOR EMPTY NESTERS

O Father, whose love remains constant even as the years bring changes to our relationship with thee, we commend empty nesters to thy providence. For faithful stewardship over long child-rearing years, bless them. In the bittersweet sending of offspring out into the world under thy hand, comfort them. And now in this new reality, redirect their lives, in vocation and avocation, and in all relationships. May they mentor young parents and families, and nurture youth in new ways. And may they all the more enter the perfect rest secured for us by our Lord Jesus Christ, who reigns with thee and the Holy Spirit, one God, in glory everlasting. *Amen.*

FOR BEFORE VISITING FAMILY FOR A HOLIDAY

Abba Father, who gathers us together as a hen gathers her brood under her wings, we commend to thee our time with family on this holiday. May we be tender with babies, playful with children, open with young folk, attentive to adults, and reverent of elders. Let us share and hear important stories. Loosen our grip on past controversies, and tighten our hold on love. Let us especially care for those whose place in our family is precarious or threatened. And make these unchosen bonds more and more chosen over time, by the grace of our Brother Jesus Christ, who gathers us to thee by the adoption of the Holy Spirit, one God, now and forever. *Amen.*

FOR THOSE FOR WHOM HOME IS NOT SAFE

O God of Hagar, Joseph, and Tamar, who prepares an everlasting home for us, we beg thee to deliver those whose homes are places of abuse, neglect, or severe dysfunction. Deploy thy mighty hand against every stronghold of evil which creates brokenness in these spaces and in these relationships. Raise up saints to provide temporary, intermittent, or permanent escape. Remove and bring abusers to justice, yet let not their victims be thus left bereft in any respect. Give thy beloved rest, therapy, and all means of recovery from trauma, and draw them speedily into the strong refuge and loving family of our Father, who reigns with the Holy Spirit and our Lord Jesus Christ, one God, now and forever. *Amen.*

FOR BEFORE PUTTING A PET DOWN

O Christ our faithful companion, who shows us a special kind of companionship through our pets, comfort and buttress our hearts as we prepare to put down our beloved buddy. Help us give full freight to the accompanying grief, and shepherd us through and past any guilt we might carry. And since thou art their first and final caretaker, take good care of them and make them new along with all things in thy new world of wildlife perfected by our Father, who reigns with thee and the Holy Spirit, one God, now and forever. *Amen.*

FOR A HAND-ME-DOWN

O Father who grafted us into the family of God and handed down to us all the riches of saintly inheritance, we give thanks for these and all hand-me-downs we have received. Thou hast allowed us to not only save money but to know whence come our possessions, to know of their past life and to give them new life; living out of an economy of communion rather than consumption. So, for repurposing these items and recycling our sorrows into triumphs, to thee and our Lord Jesus Christ and the Holy Spirit we give honor and praise, now and forever. *Amen.*

FOR STAYING AT A HAUNTED HOUSE

O Christ, who haunts the dreams of the devil and governs all souls on every plane of existence, send thy fearsome angels to stand guard with flaming swords to protect us from all haunts and hauntings of various spirits. When our observances push at the boundaries of the paranormal, still the light, sounds, and sensations we perceive. For as at thy resurrection the saints rose out of the tombs and bore witness to thy power, every being and stronghold here must yield to the name of Jesus, who reigns with our Father and the Holy Spirit, one God, in glory everlasting. *Amen.*

FOR SIBLINGS

O Christ our Brother, we pray thee to hold and shape our relationships with our siblings. Through all convergences and divergences of nature and nurture, varying degrees of closeness, and changing seasons of life, make us a memory lane and a safe home for one another. When estrangement is inevitable or necessary, soothe us, but if possible, empower us to work through every conflict and misunderstanding, that we might demonstrate to each other the steady, unconditional love of our Father, who reigns with thee and the Holy Spirit, one God, now and forever. *Amen.*

IV

THE SELF

OKAY, BEAR WITH me one more time as I talk about loneliness (*We get it, Terry, we'll call you next week*). As I was talking with my therapist (10/10, would recommend) a few weeks ago and trying to explain how I felt about living alone, an image came to me. A shooting star hurtling through space—beautiful, breathtaking, faithfully sending out a light that represents only a small part of its dynamic inner life—but only "observed" by other stars and heavenly beings for a comparatively short part of its existence.

That's what working on myself feels like much of the time. Important, often beautiful, dynamic, but unobserved in the cold vacuum of space.

The thing is, I know that married people feel like that too. Often. We all have a rich inner life, many of the countless facets of which don't necessarily become observable within the environment of intimacy. Like a shooting star hurtling through space, or one of the thousands of bonkers-looking sea creatures that we haven't discovered yet, or a moon on the other side of the galaxy, some things will only ever be seen and enjoyed and blessed by God. To the extent that I'm one of those things (which of course I'm not, but it does feel that way sometimes), I'm in excellent, glorious company.

Due to being alone a lot, I often talk to myself. When I say morning and evening prayers alone, I do those out loud as well. It keeps me from getting lost in the house of mirrors that my mind often is, yet also helps me to externalize and concretize some of the beauty of my inner life.

These prayers, I hope, are a way for you to do the same. God already puts all of our tears in a bottle, but now you might have a form by which you can also record and remember what God has seen in you and has already begun working in you toward your redemption. These collects could be the tiny pieces of paper in the bottle that represent the regrets or embarrassments that you might never share with others, or your failures that perhaps no one else will see, or your "feeling myself" moments that perhaps won't result in you getting gassed up by your friends, or your talking yourself down from responding to a troll on social media.

For some comic relief, here's the story of "For when one needs to flex on the devil after overcoming temptation." I'm at the mall to buy a new charger for my laptop. I park outside JCPenney, walk through it, and as soon as I enter the main part of the mall, there's a giant Victoria's Secret ad right in front of me. *Not today, Satan!* I avert my eyes and slide into the Apple Store. Somehow in the five minutes that I'm inside, I forget about the ad. But upon leaving, of course, there it is again. This would in many cases be the more contingent moment of temptation, but a quick "Lord, help me" and I'm through. That gets me thinking: *Hmm, we confess our sins every week in church (rightfully), but we rarely flex on the devil after we overcome temptation.* I feel like doing so would deepen our roots in holiness. You gotta learn from your defeats, but you also have to celebrate your victories, right?

Anyway, here are some collects to help you do both.

FOR WHEN ONE NEEDS TO FLEX ON THE DEVIL
AFTER OVERCOMING TEMPTATION

O Christ, who dunked on Satan thrice in the wilderness and utterly canceled him by thy death, resurrection, and inauguration, we approach thy throne of grace rejoicing that thou hast once again made us to overcome temptation. The devil tried it, truly, but thy power hath prevailed once again, to the glory of thy name, to the devastation of the flesh and all powers of evil, and to our sanctification. Thou hast taken every thought captive, preserving us from entertaining sin, and now thine angels celebrate over us, along with thou our forerunner, and our Father, and the Holy Spirit, one God, in victory unyielding. *Amen.*

FOR WHEN ONE WALKS OUT THE DOOR LOOKING FLY

O Christ, who returns in resplendent robes, let thy glory radiate out from us this day. Whether our hair be chef's kiss, our outfit fire, our scent refreshing, our nails poppin', our earrings cute, our chains low, our kicks impeccable, or our general aura a big mood, we are grateful for what we have been given. As we stunt on these unprepared souls, may they be reminded of the creative prowess of the One who crafted beauty itself, and encouraged in knowing that true artistry and exquisiteness are perceived in all by the delighted contemplation of the Holy Spirit, who reigns with thee and our Father, one God, now and forever. *Amen.*

FOR WHEN SOMETHING THROWS OFF ONE'S GROOVE

O Christ, who kept the party going when the wine ran out, give us forbearance for all manner of buzzkill. When we find ourselves by thy grace to be in good spirits, guard our joy, for between powers, principalities, and party fallacies, there are myriad forces which would seek to turn our sunny skies into shame storms. If our victory lap must be interrupted, let it be done lovingly and carefully, but if possible allow us to ride out this high all the way, with endorphins flowing as a tributary into the river of the water of life, which flows from the throne of the Father, who reigns with thee and the Holy Spirit, one God, now and forever. *Amen.*

FOR THE COME-UP

O Christ, whose final flex was ascending to heaven in the middle of conversation with thy disciples, bless all those whose glow-ups have not yet arrived or been fully realized. Like David tending the sheep, use this time to form in us the character, courage, and artistry which we will need when the time has come to step into the fullness of the thug life thou hast for us. For thou didst harrow hell and then get the party started in heaven, that we might soon say with the heavenly throng that we started from the bottom and now we're here, in the throne room of the Father, who reigns with thee and the Holy Spirit, one God, further up and further in. *Amen.*

FOR WHEN ONE FEARS GETTING CANCELED

O God who never blocks, mutes, or unfollows us but rather is the most faithful subscriber to all of our life's content, save us when the torrents of internet cancellation threaten to roll over us. When we fear that our hot take may have been too spicy, or that our words or intentions might be misinterpreted, make us both sensitive and secure. Make us open to genuine pushback, and willing to correct or delete Web postings, yet kindly protect us from dunks and subtweets. And though we oft say "And I oop," let thy grace swoop in and gather us to our Father, who reigns with our Lord Jesus Christ and the Holy Spirit, one God, now and forever. *Amen.*

FOR WRESTLING WITH DOUBT

O Savior who upon the cross proclaimed, "My God, my God, why hast thou forsaken me?," make thyself known to those who struggle with doubt. When we doubt thy realness, graciously evidence thy presence in our lives and in our world. When we doubt thy goodness, show love to us, and enable us to receive it. When we doubt thy capacity, act in, through, and for us. Dialogue with our questions, give us friends who are paragons of faith, and ultimately cultivate in us a trust which surpasses understanding in the Father in whom we are rooted, who reigns with thee and the Holy Spirit, one God, now and forever. *Amen.*

FOR WHEN PLANS ARE SUSPENDED OR LOST

O Christ, infinitely resourceful to redeem all of our losses, carry us now. That which could and should have been has been snatched away, leaving us hollow and disoriented. The ground has been pulled out from under us—rescue us from this freefall. For every marriage postponed, commencement canceled, project fizzled out, job lost, and dream deferred, give us the physical, mental, and emotional space to grieve, as we cling to the laments of our forebears. And in due time fill this void with the boundless creative and restorative prowess of the Holy Spirit, who reigns with thee and our Father, one God, in glory untold. *Amen.*

FOR BEFORE ENTERING A PUBLIC RESTROOM

O God our cleanser, whose baptismal font is the true baby changing station, protect us as we enter and utilize this public restroom. As thou art our buffer against various forms of evil, be the same between us and this toilet seat and all other germ repositories. Let the toilet paper, like thy mercies, not run out on us, and let this restroom have the good hand dryers whose streams make glad the people of God. Make soap, privacy, and no-touch technology plentiful, that we might do our business and then quickly return to being about the business of our Father, who reigns with our Lord Jesus Christ and the Holy Spirit, one God, now and forever. *Amen.*

FOR WHEN ONE REMEMBERS AN EMBARRASSMENT
FROM THE PAST

O Father who out of time, redemption, and formation crafts a balm to soothe the wounds of our past, govern our thoughts. Thou hast given us wisdom where there was naivete, prudence where there was folly, and sophistication where there was basicness. So let this remembrance serve not to tear us down but rather to build us up in the knowledge of how thou hast atoned for our mistakes, humbled us to find amusement in our foibles, and changed us since then for the better. And by thy grace we will present ourselves to thee as those approved by our Lord Jesus Christ, who reigns with thee and the Holy Spirit, one God, in glory everlasting. *Amen.*

FOR WHEN SET ROUTINES ARE DISLODGED

O Father whose providence accounts for all the vicissitudes of our lives, thou hast helped us to construct routines which engender good habits, take much of the guesswork out of our daily movements, and anchor us when other things are in flux. Yet now we lament our loss of this stability. Kindly protect our mental health in this time. Give us creativity and discipline to construct new routines which retain much from before and even form us in new ways. Make us as consistent in our sleeping, eating, working, and loving as possible, as we lean on Jesus Christ our solid rock, who reigns with thee and the Holy Spirit, one God, now and forever. *Amen.*

FOR STORY WORK

O Word of God, assist us as we seek to remember, reframe, reverse, reimagine, and renarrate our lives. By thy beautiful design, our realities are organized and maintained by stories. By thy grace, we are not our problem narratives—help us to externalize them, deconstruct them, and map their tactics and effects. Reveal to us exceptions and subplots in which we have experienced thy deliverance, and help us to thicken them. Give us new language, new interpretive lenses, and a reconstructed worldview, for the glory of our Father, who makes us co-authors along with thee and the Holy Spirit, one God, story without end. *Amen.*

FOR WHEN ONE REALIZES THAT GOD BLOCKED IT

O God our shield, who knows what we do and do not need when we cannot, we recognize that thou hast closed doors which we so deeply wanted to pass through, and now we are so glad that thou didst so. In the infinite foresight of thy providence and grace, thou hast kept us from those attractive opportunities which would not have been best for us, and in many cases may even have been destructive for us. Do bring this to our remembrance when in the future we bristle at the "no" of our Lord Jesus Christ, who reigns with thee our Father and the Holy Spirit, one God, world without end. *Amen.*

FOR COMING OUT

O Christ, whose redemption reconciles us to ourselves and to one another, we pray thy protection and quickening upon those who have recently or will shortly come out. Thou hast governed the development of their sexuality and integrated their faith, conscience, and identity. We rejoice in the flourishing this may allow, and the fruit it will bear for thy kingdom. Soften and change the hearts of those who cannot or will not yet understand. And give these thy beloved a coherence of mind, body, gender, and sexuality in the abundant life provided by the Holy Spirit, who reigns with thee and our Father, one God, in glory everlasting. *Amen.*

FOR ONE'S CELEBRITY CRUSH

O Famous One, we entreat thy blessing upon our celebrity crushes. Their work has inspired us, their words encouraged us, and their aesthetic delighted us in ways that have brought to mind the glory that thy grace will one day bestow upon us all. Protect them, draw them unto thyself, and if it please thee, arrange in thy providence for our bespoke encounter with them. And may they ultimately remind us to always be fangirls of our Lord Jesus Christ, who reigns with our Father and the Holy Spirit, one God, in eternal renown. *Amen.*

FOR AN ENCOUNTER WITH LAW ENFORCEMENT

O Spirit our shield, we ask thy grace over this interaction. Grace it with a spirit of compassion and understanding.

Preserve it from escalation, unnecessary verbal or physical force, racism, and any other abuse of power. Help this officer to discharge their duty to protect and serve, and help us to receive a fair or even merciful adjudication. Order this interaction toward our safety and the safety of those sharing public spaces with us, by the protection of our Father, who reigns with thee and our Lord Jesus Christ, one God, in perfect peace. *Amen.*

FOR THOSE EXPERIENCING SUICIDAL IDEATION

O Lover whose image we bear, whose estimation of us is incalculable, sing sweetly to the souls of those for whom life feels unbearable. Bring quickly those who will grieve with them, stay with them, and seek to understand and bear their burdens. Let therapy guide them through steps to heal from abandonment, grief, self-loathing, or trauma. When the present seems to be a wasteland, and the future a dark void, give them a bright spot which lights one step of the path. Do so again and again; shepherd them away from death into the life of the Holy Spirit, who reigns with the Father and our Lord Jesus Christ, one God, in radiance everlasting. *Amen.*

FOR FOMO

O God who perceives all things, we entreat thee for respite from the fear of missing out. Console us in our feelings of regret and lack. Make us to sit in our finitude, and there find rest and dependence on thee. Show us the futility of wondering what could or might have been. And help us to be content in, and make the most of, the select things we have chosen to partake of. For thy love and governance through these things are all we need, by the design of our Father, who reigns with the Holy Spirit and our Lord Jesus Christ, one God, now and forever. *Amen.*

FOR MEMORY WORK

O God of profound thought, whose knowledge of all moments is perfect, aid us in our putting a sponge to the past. Help us to soak up all that which will illuminate our present and our future. Make synapses fire which make crisp memories long submerged. Show us their interconnections, and kindly build them into a scaffolding and a metanarrative for our lives. May we name the pain and the wrong therein, and thus know how to fight it and heal from it. And make us feel the joy therein. All this for the remembrance of our Lord Jesus Christ, who reigns with the Father and the Holy Spirit, one God, now and forever. *Amen.*

FOR WHEN ONE IS RECEIVING UNWANTED MALE ATTENTION

Jehovah Nissi, raise thy banner of love and protection over us now. Restore to us the peace taken from us by violence and trauma, and dissolve the false guilt which the Accuser would have us to hold. Rebuke and visit justice upon abusive men and patriarchal principalities. Turn bystanders into conscientious interveners, both now and in our streets, trains, schools, workplaces, and policy-making rooms more broadly, by the power of our Lord Jesus Christ, who reigns with our Father and the Holy Spirit, one God, in perfect righteousness. *Amen.*

FOR WHEN IT IS DIFFICULT TO PRAY

O Spirit who intercedes for us with groans that words cannot express—our desire, willingness, or facility for prayer fails us in this moment. At times we seek to be far removed from thee. At times we are angry or apathetic toward thee. At times we want to pray, but no words come. By clarion call beckon us from these places into thy throne room, if for no other purpose than to sit and listen. And as we do, restore to us the words of life by which we might articulate our thoughts and feelings to thee once again. For God alone our souls in stillness wait—truly our hope is in thee who reigns, Father, Son, and Holy Spirit, one God, in heedfulness unremitting. *Amen.*

FOR THE MOMENT OF ANGER OR FRUSTRATION

O Holy Spirit, sovereign over our emotions, pull us away from the brink. Breath of God, fill us as we pause to inhale and exhale. Affirm that in us which is rightfully hurt or angry. Help us think and speak productively, attacking the problem, not the person. Flush the pride out of our system, that in our anger we might not sin. Save us from the perverted pleasure offered by acrimony. And let thy sanctifying work in us prevail once again, for the peace of our Lord Jesus Christ, the honor of the Father, and the blessing of the Spirit, one God, now and forever. *Amen.*

FOR DECISIVENESS

O God of endless possibility, giver and sustainer of our freedom, we praise thee for the opportunities thou hast provided us, and the decisions that thou hast given us to make. Yet we lament that we are so often indecisive; given to paralysis by analysis. Our minds run wild with worst-case scenarios, imagined butterfly effects, or simple fear of the unknown. But thou hast not given us a spirit of fear, but of power, and of love, and of a sound mind. So, Spirit of discernment, graciously lead us to the best, or better, or good, or even *a* decision that we may trust is in alignment with the providence of our Father, who reigns with thee and our Lord Jesus Christ, one God, now and forever. *Amen.*

FOR THOSE STRUGGLING WITH OR RECOVERING FROM EATING DISORDERS

O God of restoration, we pray for those whose relationship with food is fraught. Make us sympathetic to the deep-seated nature of this struggle with such a constant and fundamental part of life. Touch these thy beloved, and for them make food a sacrament whereby they take in the fruit of thy world and turn it back into worship of thee. We ask thee to rebuke, dismantle, and destroy all powers and principalities of distorted self-image, unhealthy beauty conventions, and self-harm. Give thy children treatment, therapy, support, and endurance for the long road of recovery, that they may taste and see that the Lord Jesus Christ is good, in the sweetness of the Holy Spirit and the satisfaction of the Father, one God, now and forever. *Amen.*

FOR TIMES OF DEPRESSION

O Christ, who on earth knew an isolating, obscure, persistent sorrow, we seek thy solace for those experiencing depression. When all we see is hardship, be the lifter of our heads, and show us the radiance of thy countenance beholding us with delight. When all we feel is heaviness, be the bearer of our burdens, and show our hearts an unexpected levity. While we boldly ask for deliverance, in the meantime we ask thy help in adjusting. May medication and therapy touch our minds, faithful friends bear up our souls, and may our strength once again be the joy of our Lord Jesus Christ, who reigns with the Father and the Holy Spirit, one God, in triumph everlasting. *Amen.*

FOR MOVING TO A NEW PLACE

O itinerant Christ, well acquainted with the feeling of rootlessness, we ask for thy guidance as we settle into the new place to which thou hast brought us. We thank thee for the goodness of this place, which is already apparent. We do lament that which from our former place has been uprooted— cherished relationships, meaningful work, beloved spaces, and more. Kindly transplant us deeply into this new soil. Give us new friends who are present, available, and loving. Give us new rhythms and a heart for this new place, and show us where thou art at work here, reigning with the Father and the Holy Spirit, one God, now and forever. *Amen.*

FOR WHEN ONE IS GETTING TROLLED ONLINE

O Prince of Peace, deft handler of situations in which folks set out to entrap or get a rise out of thee, we beseech thee for a divine unbotheredness with respect to hecklers. Help us to pick our battles wisely, and perhaps none of the online variety. Do preserve us from the urge to carry out arguments in our head, and let us always respond to misplaced contempt with the well-placed dignity of our Lord Jesus Christ, who reigns with the Father and the Holy Spirit, one God, now and forever. *Amen.*

FOR TIMES OF ISOLATION

O God of John the Divine, Athanasius, and Julian of Norwich, who never leaves nor forsakes us, demonstrate thy friendship to us now. Speak to us in a voice more audible than ever before, and touch us with a sensation more palpable. Let us approach silence and solitude as spiritual disciplines by which we may be formed into thy likeness. If possible, give us the means to contact friends and family, and through restorative interaction fill us with a deep sense of being known and cherished. And hasten the time when we may once again be among the loved ones given to us by our Father, who reigns with the Holy Spirit and our Lord Jesus Christ, one God, present now and forever. *Amen.*

FOR BEFORE GETTING ONE'S HAIR CUT

O God who has counted all the hairs on our heads, be gracious to us as we entrust our crown of glory to our barbers and stylists. Kindly make our fades fresh as thy daily mercies, our braids strong as three-strand cords, our twists tight as thy preserving hold upon the saints, and our hairlines crisp and straight as the narrow path of righteousness. May the barbershop be our sanctuary, our spa, and our cultural watering hole, and may looking good lead to our feeling good and then our doing good for the kingdom of our Lord Jesus Christ, who reigns with thee and the Holy Spirit, one God, now and forever. *Amen.*

FOR WHEN ONE CANNOT GET TO THE BARBER/HAIRSTYLIST

O Spirit who anoints our head with precious oil, be not only the lifter but also the styler of our head in times when we have no recourse to our barbers and hairdressers. When the back of our head is ridiculous, teach us the basics of self-service, or give us the immense fortitude to entrust a member of our household with the clippers. And because the half-life of our freshness is short, show us low-maintenance/low-reward hairstyles for this time, for the glory of our Lord Jesus Christ, for whom we are high-maintenance/high-reward objects of sanctification, who reigns with thee and our Father, one God, now and forever. *Amen.*

FOR ADULTING

O Mother whose eye is on the sparrow, and upon us as we leave the nest and later begin to make nests of our own, as thou hast raised our spirits raise also our credit scores. As our overhead increases and our margin of error decreases, navigate us through uncharted seas of budgeting, insurance, home furnishing, and all manner of self-reliance. And let our independence grow commensurately with our dependence on thee, who paid our existential bills and funded our eschatological retirement plans with the riches won by our Ransom Jesus Christ, who reigns with thee and the Holy Spirit, one God, world without end. *Amen.*

FOR CULTURAL HUMILITY

O Holy Spirit, the tonic for toxicity and the repairer of fragility, we beseech thee for a radically humble and contrite spirit with which to approach cross-cultural encounter. Reveal our privilege, unconscious bias, and blind spots to us, and make us heartbroken at the ways in which they are evidences of a broken world. Give us capacity to engage new perspectives, receptiveness to rebuke, resources with which to educate ourselves, and resolution to become better allies through the sanctifying work of our Savior Jesus Christ, who reigns with thee and our Father, one God, in perfect solidarity. *Amen.*

FOR WHEN ONE NEEDS TO FLEE TEMPTATION

O God our safe retreat, who made Joseph fleet of foot to escape evil, give us the nerve to protect and swerve. Though the flesh would have us to cha-cha slide down the slippery slope, help us to reverse, reverse—neither entertaining nor engaging sin, that we might not half-step but rather high-step over obstacles and hightail it out of the danger zone. For the devil is cursed to eat our dust as we run like the wind toward the bull's-eye of the glory of our forerunner Jesus Christ, who reigns with the Father and the Holy Spirit, one God, world without end. *Amen.*

FOR BEFORE FLYING

O Christ, who never loses us thy luggage but always checks and secures the bag, who made our redemption a personal item and our hope a carry-on to thine ascension, it is by thy sanctification that we are in an upright and locked position. For as we now traverse this layover between the already and not yet, thy providence is the Chili's Too which sustains us unto our final departure out of this liminal space. And thy blood is the TSA pre-check which clears us for approach to the Father, who reigns with thee and the Holy Spirit, one God, now and forever. *Amen.*

FOR WHEN ONE HAS JUST COME INTO SOME MONEY

O God who makes it rain blessings upon us daily, we seek to steward little and much with equal care. So as thou didst treat thyself in creating the untold beauty of the cosmos, show us the right items to purchase from our disposable income wish list. Guide our budgeting, our saving, our investing, and our ongoing resistance to consumerism and capitalism, that even when we be flush with cash, we might not be crushed by brash powers of mammon but rather beholden only to the laws of generosity and gratitude unto our Lord Jesus Christ, who reigns with thee and the Holy Spirit, one God, now and forever. *Amen.*

FOR THE AMBIVALENTLY ATTACHED

O God, whose attachment to us knows no measure or fluctuation, restore relational hope to the ambivalently attached. We grieve the inconsistent or distorted caregiving that contributed to this mechanism of survival. Show them thine immediate response to their every slightest pain and anxious feeling. Validate their needs through relationships whose sweet security precludes asymmetry, clinging, and over-attuning. Break every feedback cycle of isolation, rejection, and abandonment, and reconstruct a psychology of trust through the hope deposited in us by the Holy Spirit, who reigns with thee and our Lord Jesus Christ, one God, now and forever. *Amen.*

FOR THOSE WHO EXPERIENCE OBSESSIONS AND/OR COMPULSIONS

O Christ, master of the waves which toss and roar and yet cannot transgress the boundaries you set, call out to the mind assailed by obsessions and compulsions. Draw lines to circumscribe the excess and power of unwanted thoughts and feelings. Within those limits, show us an acceptance that is its own resistance, and a patience that is its own perfection, and a reserve of grace for oneself in the storehouses of our Father who reigns with thee and the Holy Spirit, one God, now and forever. *Amen.*

FOR WAITING

O Christ, who waited thirty years before entering thy
ministry, who sanctifies us through holy anticipation—
help us to wait well. Make us wait actively, like Paul and
Silas ministering and attending to the Lord, standing by for
deliverance. Make us wait faithfully over long years, like Anna
and Simeon. Make our daily-repeated petitions effective.
Shape us especially when we cannot perceive thy working.
And attune us all the more to thy timing and thy will for our
longings, that we may come to expect the fulfillment of all
holy desire by the consummation of thy kingdom, thine along
with the Father and the Holy Spirit, one God, world without
end. *Amen.*

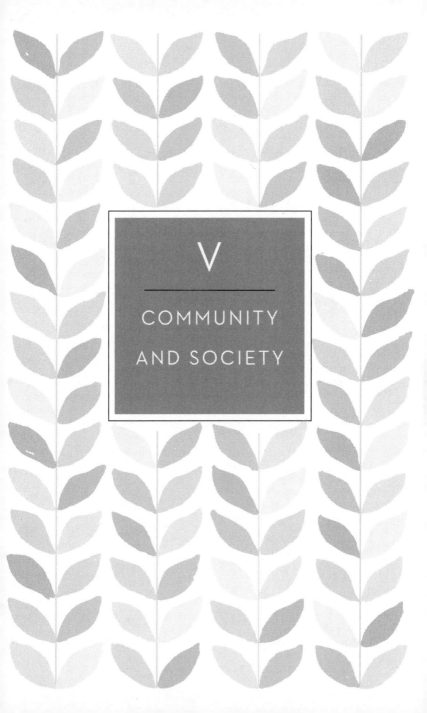

V

COMMUNITY
AND SOCIETY

I'M IN A youth ministers' group text made up of classmates from seminary. A couple of weeks ago, around the time of the 2020 presidential election, one of my good friends asked the group, "Is anyone else working in a place where you're being asked not to post anything that 'shows your cards' politically on social media?" A few days later another person asked, "Sooooooo, how might you respond to a student who says 'no matter who wins, Jesus is on the throne' in a church context where you've been told not to show your cards?"

I did eventually respond in a helpful way to my friends, but I gotta be honest, my first reaction was [insert Kermit-drinking-tea meme]: "Whew, couldn't be me!"

I'm privileged to be the youth minister at a church that does refugee resettlement, anti-trafficking, immigration advocacy, anti-incarceration, anti-racism, mental health services, drop-in legal services, and so much more. The corresponding Bible verses are on signs lining the hallways and even the murals on the outside of the building. After three years of deconstruction and reconstruction in seminary, in which I could only imagine the kind of church that might reflect the things that I was learning and unlearning, I was placed into a congregation that embodied all of that and more.

And the timing couldn't have been better, as the apocalyptic reckoning of this year has awoken many and radicalized some when it comes to justice, including me. Before this year, I thought "f#@! tha Police" was a song that I had no connection to; after the murder of George Floyd, I realized that it was a real movement with history, theory, and data to back up its message that the American institution of police has always only protected the interests of rich whites at the expense of the poor, especially BIPOC, and has been so steeped in this original sin that it is unreformable.

BEING ABLE TO turn "abolish the police," "eat the rich," "save the earth," and other cries of my generation into collects—pulling easily from the words of Jesus and the prophets and the psalmists—was my way of channeling my rage, despair, and hope as I cycled through these feelings, often carrying all at once.

It was also draining. I was so blessed to watch my colleague and publishing housemate Cole Arthur Riley step into liturgical leadership in these areas, and to be filled and inspired by her words in the same way that mine have done for others.

Many of these prayers are more evergreen, more light-hearted, or more mundane than the ones that came specifically out of the 2020 upswell of the Black Lives Matter movement. But I hope that all carry the same potential to grow our awareness of others, and help congeal the collective consciousness about issues that affect all of us.

FOR ENTERING A NEW YEAR

O Alpha and Omega, who maketh all things new, we commend this new year to thy sustaining and transforming power. Give us hindsight as we examine our victories, failures, joys, and heartbreaks from this past year. Give us foresight to envision how we might grow more into thy likeness in this new year. And bless us with accountability and discipline to keep resolutions, strength to move on from past failures, and a resolve to make each new day and every moment holy unto our Lord Jesus Christ, who reigns with thee and the Holy Spirit, one God, now and forever. *Amen.*

FOR ECONOMIC JUSTICE

O Christ, who fills the hungry with good things and sends the rich away empty, melt down and reshape our economy. Conquer the powers of exploitation, privilege, and resentment which rule us now, and as righteous victor plunder the stolen and hoarded wealth of corporations, Wall Street, the rich, and the systems that prop them up. Pour all of it into reparations, fair trade, workers' rights, healthcare, education, housing, infrastructure, and other social programs determined by our communities themselves. For thou art the Way out of economic death into abundant life, reigning with our Father and the Holy Spirit, one God, now and forever. *Amen.*

FOR DIVESTMENT FROM POLICE

O God of restorative justice, sovereign to dismantle entrenched sin, continue to expose the evil of policing in this country. Redirect this nation's wealth away from police, prisons, and a corrupt judicial system, and toward community initiatives in healthcare, education, housing, employment, and other services which address the core of the inequity whence come crime and disorder. Show restoration to be more effective than punishment, and help us see people not as problems to manage but as image-bearers to invest in, per the command of our Lord Jesus Christ, who reigns with thee and the Holy Spirit, one God, now and forever. *Amen.*

FOR YOUTHS NAVIGATING AND RESISTING RACISM

O Christ, whose kingdom belongs to the children and the childlike, restore the youth stolen from Black and brown kids in racist America. Heal the developmental, generational, and genetic trauma caused by both the overt and the subtler violence of anti-Blackness. Be a refuge for parents as they seek to be such for their children, and fortify their family systems and their communities' cohesion. Make white youths' formation anti-racist. And let what our young people inherit from us be a new society; new life birthed and nurtured by our Mother who reigns with thee and the Holy Spirit, one God, now and forever. *Amen.*

FOR AFTER A LYNCHING

O Christ, enthroned on the seat of judgment, enraged by the abominations of racism and murder—we cry out with inflamed tongues and pierced hearts—save us! Is there no respite from the gaze which sees Black life as unworthy, from the hands that discard our lives, from the entrenched sin of a nation, from the evil built into our very psyche? Will they visit upon the thousandth generation? Maranatha, Lord! Let thine anger burn hot to bring a reckoning upon this anathema, and justice upon all who with contempt snuff out the lives of those who are unspeakably loved by our Father, who reigns with thee and the Holy Spirit, one God, to make all things right. *Amen.*

FOR A PROTEST

O Judge of the world, to whom vengeance belongs, who casts down the mighty from their thrones and lifts up the lowly, take up our cause. Rise up for us against the wicked, the powers of evil whose unconscionable injustices have brought us to and past our breaking point. Hold up our arms as we raise signs, amplify our voices as we chant and sing refrains of righteousness, protect us from danger, and make the force of our will stronger than the inertia of the status quo. Let God arise, and let God's enemies be scattered by the power of our Lord Jesus Christ, who reigns with the Father and the Holy Spirit, one God, here and now. *Amen.*

FOR BIG STRUCTURAL CHANGE

O God of the remnant, who breaks down and builds up again, we need to be reborn. Send the angel of death to slay the systems and institutions which drain and destroy our lives— not least an economy which sacrifices us on the altar of profit, and a culture which sacrifices Black and brown bodies on the altar of white supremacy. Burn them down, O Consuming Fire, and gather together a people who are led by thy Spirit to build new and equitable systems out of the rubble, through Jesus Christ our Lord, who reigns with thee and the Holy Spirit, one God, here and now. *Amen.*

FOR US TO BE RADICALIZED

O Holy Spirit—the fire shut up in our bones, bestowing prophetic utterance out of the overflow of overwhelmed hearts—awaken us! Let the cries of our siblings' blood rise from the earth in a whirlwind, catching us up in divine fury. Reveal to us, and divest us from, the deeply evil narratives and systems which underpin our collective life. Let thy word filter the ideas, images, and experiences through which we are destabilized, reeducated, and re-formed as those who are ready to be led in a radical exodus by our Lord Jesus Christ, who reigns with thee and our Father, one God, in power made perfect by love. *Amen.*

FOR VOTING

O Christ, who served humbly and led radically, whose redemption sets forth the world we envision when we vote, govern our choices and amplify our voices. Shape our conscience to thy will; show us what justice and love require of us in this moment. Triumph over voter suppression and underrepresentation, and abolish all electoral structures which undermine our votes. Help us to hold our leaders accountable in other ways, as part of our witness to the ultimate lordship of our Sovereign who reigns with thee and the Holy Spirit, one God, now and forever. *Amen.*

FOR BLACK JOY

O Wonderful Counselor, who sings sweetly to our souls, descend upon us and reaffirm that we are thy beloved children with whom thou art well pleased. As the sun hath kissed our skin, so kiss our faces with the lips that call us Black and beautiful. Though powers not only hate us but also work hard to make us hate ourselves, we recall thy faithfulness by which we wrought true faith out of the dead religion of slavers, profound artistry out of pain, and beautiful culture out of the Black joy which overcomes by the blood of the Lamb, the Word of our testimony, who reigns with thee and our Father, one God, in glory everlasting. *Amen.*

FOR THE GOOD GIFT OF SEXUALITY

O intimate Spirit, we praise thee for endowing us with, and helping us express beautifully, our sexuality. Uproot the deep-seated fear, shame, silence, and misinformation in which, for many of us, sex has been enshrouded. Reeducate us, appropriately to our need, in the wondrous physiological, psychological, interpersonal, and theological realities of sexual intimacy. Help us construct an ethic based on holistic care, self-mastery, and all other fruits and freedoms of the Spirit. And refine our every desire in the fire of the passionate love of our Father, who reigns with thee and our Lord Jesus Christ, one God, now and forever. *Amen.*

FOR THOSE EXPERIENCING GENDER DYSPHORIA

O God who is sovereign over our nature and our nurture, we lift up those who experience gender dysphoria. Let any nonconformity be met with acceptance, questioning with openness, and their undertaking of inner and outer changes with support. Do the hard, gradual work of changing the hearts of family and friends who cannot or will not do so. And give them all that they need to achieve resonance between body, mind, and soul, that they might know the shalom of our God who is genderless, and also the fullness of all that gender can signify, made known to us in Jesus Christ by the Holy Spirit, one God, now and forever. *Amen.*

FOR FIGHTING BEAUTYISM

O Father to whose beauty our souls are drawn, help us come to know and love thee so intimately that we cannot help but see thy glory in every person we encounter. Make us ever aware of the insidious temptation to treat better, seek out more, or value higher those whom we find aesthetically attractive. Help us to fight against the conventions and structures built to propagate the mentality and practice of beautyism in our culture. Give us a glimpse of thy vision and a taste of thy delight in beholding each of thy creatures, of whose worth the source is Jesus Christ, who reigns with thee and the Holy Spirit, one God, now and forever. *Amen.*

FOR SUMMERTIME

O Christ of open-toed shoes, who stretches forth thy hand to bring the skies out that we might in turn have our thighs out, whose love covers and protects us better than SPF 100, we seek nothing more than to boogie board on the waves of thy grace. So let this summer replenish not only our vitamin D but also our vitamin JC, and whether we be beach babes or sk8er bois, help us to feel the summer breeze of the Holy Spirit, who reigns with thee and our Father, one God, in everlasting warmth and radiance. *Amen.*

FOR THE HATERS

O Christ who looked on the haters with love, but also stunted on them, we commend to thee all who drink haterade. Make us receptive to the real ones who bring genuine constructive criticism, but when folks come out of the woodwork to keep us from doing our thing, prepare a force field and a three-course meal for us in the presence of our enemies, and keep our minds on that which is lovely and praiseworthy. Haters will say it's Photoshop, but make us bear the image of the One who got 'em with the resurrection and ascension, whose thug life is also a hug life, who reigns with our Father and the Holy Spirit, one God, now and forever. *Amen.*

FOR THOSE WHO ARE BEING BULLIED

O Christ our champion, who endured insult, threat, and hatred from one-time and repeat offenders alike, dismantle the structures and principalities of bullying in our culture. Give victims a safe way to tell peers and authorities what's going on, and may the latter be quick to provide support and justice. Through friends, mentors, and thy Spirit, speak words of affirmation which resound so loudly and clearly in their soul so as to expunge all destructive messages. And give them an unshakable assurance that they are invaluable and loved by our Father, who reigns with thee and the Holy Spirit, one God, mighty fortress. *Amen.*

FOR A PANDEMIC

O Healer of all creation, we come to lay our fears and confusion at the foot of thy throne. As this illnesss spreads, shine thy light perpetual on those who have died, and be a stronghold for those at risk. Give supernatural endurance, ingenuity, and dexterity to all public health officials and hospital personnel. Give public servants wisdom for the tough decisions they now must make. Redeem our lost time, resources, and plans, and provide for those who cannot afford these disruptions. And turn this chaos into order for the kingdom of our Lord Jesus Christ, who reigns with our Father and the Holy Spirit, one God, now and forever. *Amen.*

FOR A WOMAN PRESIDENT

O God of Deborah, Huldah, and Esther, our hearts are heavy. The principalities of sexism and androcentrism seem to prevail no matter how eminently capable or even undeniably superior our women candidates are. We long for a president who operates out of a woman's perspective, resilience, and wisdom. We long for young women to see themselves represented in the highest office. Sow the seeds of big structural change in this nation, that after a long struggle our eyes might see what we have hoped for, by the power of the One who sits on the throne, and Christ the Lamb, and the Holy Spirit, one God, now and forever. *Amen.*

FOR EMOTIONALLY COMPETENT MEN

O Father who trains us up in the way we should go, we pray thee to raise up men who are emotionally deft and aware. Help us to listen, cry, empathize, and know ourselves, like Jesus. Make us tender like Jonathan, demonstrative like John, and happy standing behind and beside powerful women, like Aquila. And dismantle the principalities of toxic masculinity which reward us for doing the opposite, that we may grow up into the stature of emotional richness of our Lord Jesus Christ, who reigns with thee and the Holy Spirit, one God, now and forever. *Amen.*

FOR WHEN ONE HEARS AN AMBULANCE

O God our Rescuer, graciously make haste to help those to whom these responders are on their way. Clear traffic for the latter, and give them wisdom and a calm hand to resolve any danger. Preserve the life and safety of the former—if they have sustained injuries, give them quick passage to the hospital, and excellent care. For it is thou who takes us out of harm's way, by the grace of our Lord Jesus Christ, who reigns with the Father and the Holy Spirit, one God, in health and peace everlasting. *Amen.*

FOR THE WINTER

O God who exfoliates our skin and our sin—as thou dost bless the earth with the morning dew, so renew the health of our bodies in this season of dryness and earthly quietus. When the sun hides her face from us for weeks on end, rejuvenate our minds to save us from seasonal downswings. May the dull landscape remind us of thy faithfulness in the humdrum times of life. Wrap us in the layers of thy loving-kindness, and may we there be warmed until the spring returns and we rise like a phoenix out of the ashiness, as didst our Lord Jesus Christ, who reigns with the Father and the Holy Spirit, one God, now and in all seasons. *Amen.*

FOR CANCELLATION OF STUDENT LOAN DEBT

O Lord of the year of Jubilee, who eradicates the deepest and most existential of debts, we long and hope for the cancellation of our student loan debt. Let such discourse continue to advance in the public square. Let proper strategies take hold in the minds, words, and policies of public servants. Let the lobbies and corporations which stand to lose profit be undermined in their resistance, and let this burden be lifted off of us, that we might receive economic power to put to work for ourselves, our families, and our communities, by the grace and deliverance of our Lord Jesus Christ, who reigns with the Father and the Holy Spirit, one God, world without end. *Amen.*

FOR WHEN WAR IS THREATENED

O Lamb of God, who resisted empire to the point of death and sets us at peace with God, we fervently implore thee to rebuke and destroy all powers and principalities of violence, self-interest, and injustice which threaten to lead us into war. We beseech thee to de-escalate tensions, govern the deliberations of our political and military leaders toward prudence, and reveal to us another way forward. Let us be especially governed by concern for the poor and vulnerable. Hasten the coming of thy reign of peace, into which all the nations will bring their splendor, where we will beat our swords into plowshares, and where all are reconciled under the lordship of Jesus Christ, in the holy Zion of our Father and the unity of the Holy Spirit, one God, in glory everlasting. *Amen.*

FOR AFTER A TRAGIC OR SUDDEN DEATH

O Lord, who when the foundations are rent asunder, and the righteous know not what to do, continues to reign from thy holy temple, we beg thee to shine thy light perpetual on [name], taken from us tragically. There is no sense in this disaster; we are shell-shocked. We are gutted, with no words—only tears. How long, O Lord? Hasten the ultimate perishing of death; the eradication of loss by thy renewal of all things. Comfort us all, especially those closest to the departed. Hide them in the shadow of thy wings, and be their unshakable refuge in this grief, by the consolation of the Holy Spirit, who lives and reigns with the Father and our Lord Jesus Christ, one God, in redemption unfolding. *Amen.*

FOR ALLIES OF FOLKS WITH DISABILITIES

O Christ, impaired in body, disabled by society, we lift up to thee our disabled neighbors. We grieve and repent of the ways in which we have taken away agency, defined people by their impairments, and centered ourselves as superior and normative. Show us how to sit at the feet of these thy beloved, to give their experiences and ideas overriding weight, and to support their movement for equity. And as thou hast expanded the family of God on our behalf, show us how to expand the range of abilities which we accommodate fully in our society, for thy glory, reigning with the Father and the Holy Spirit, one God, now and forever. *Amen.*

FOR ONE'S ONLINE COMMUNITY

O Lord of the Interwebs, who added us to the professional network of believers, we pray thy blessing upon our online communities. We praise thee for creating a space wherein we may find healthy discourse, personal encouragement, and genuine friendships—we recognize that these are hard to come by. Deepen our impact, that we may learn, include, and bless more. May we be slow to dunk, and quick to meme, that we might increase, in the world and in the World Wide Web, the followers of our Lord Jesus Christ, who reigns with the Father and the Holy Spirit, one God, in glory everlasting. *Amen.*

FOR BLACK SELF-LOVE

O prismatic Godhead, who delights to create and sustain the beauty of Blackness, we commend our community to thee. We give thanks for the saintly communion we enjoy with our ancestors, who gave their all that we might have a better life. We ask thy grace and providence over the work of all anti-racist activists, organizers, and institutions. Now help us to love ourselves profoundly, and to see how we uniquely image God. Dismantle and free us from the principalities of white normativity, colorism, and internalized racism. And help us to edify and magnify, rather than police and gatekeep, each other's Blackness, building each other up in the love of the Father, Spirit, and dark-hued Jesus Christ, one God, in glory everlasting. *Amen.*

FOR BLACK GIRLS AND BLACK WOMEN

O God of Hagar, Felicity, and Sojourner, thou hast graced us with these beloved who show forth thy glory in a unique and brilliant way. Make us sensitive to the compounding natures of sexism, racism, and colorism, and enlist us in thy campaign against these principalities. Make us to recognize the strength of Black women without caricaturing them as superheroes.

Make us vocal allies against their defamation, not least by believing them and sitting at their feet. Help us recognize and name their beauty, and let Black Girl Magic always turn us in wonder to thee our Mother who reigns with our Lord Jesus Christ and the Holy Spirit, one God, in perfect majesty. *Amen.*

FOR WHEN PEOPLE ARE BEING RUDE IN PUBLIC

O Christ, who loved the masses yet withdrew for respite, we request thy fortitude now with respect to tactless and inconsiderate behavior in this public space. Assist us in tuning out overly loud phone talkers or audio listeners. Remove from us those who encroach upon our personal space. If we must call anyone out, let us do so respectfully and firmly. And may our God spread conviction and repentance upon all manspreaders, that we may sit comfortably in thy governance over our going out and our coming in, by the providence of our Father, who reigns with thee and the Holy Spirit, one God, now and forever. *Amen.*

FOR THE DISCOURSE AROUND A MOVEMENT

O Christ, who in righteous anger often lifted thy voice in rebuke and holy disruption, sanctify our discourse. Focus it, that we might converge on the issues at hand like many streams flowing into one rushing rapid. Channel our upwelling emotion into proclamation which draws truth-seekers in and makes the devil flee. Give us a keen eye for misinformation and propaganda, wisdom in curating our social media feeds, humility to recant and change after learning new and better information, and bravery to document and broadcast the evils of our adversaries and the liberating power of the Holy Spirit, who reigns with thee and our Mother, one God, here and now. *Amen.*

FOR POLITICAL LEADERS DURING A MOVEMENT

O Christ, our king who rides out in front of us as we battle the forces of evil, light a fire under our elected officials and public servants, that they might fall in where and how thou art moving through us. Fill their inboxes and phone lines with our demands, and their minds with strategies for how to support and enact them. Make them forego virtue signals for principled stands, even at the expense of political expediency, or of their jobs. Cut through conflicts of interest, red tape, and all obstacles to radical change with the sword of the Spirit, who reigns with thee and our Father, one God, above all earthly powers. *Amen.*

FOR SUSTAINED ENERGY FOR A MOVEMENT

O Sustaining Spirit, who renews the strength of those who wait upon thee, we claim thy promise that we will run and not be weary, that we will walk and not faint. Keep our foot on the gas and our hands to the task of liberation. Use us like a tag team to relieve our co-laborers. When one divine display starts to fade, give us another victory. When support seems to dwindle, close our ranks, and plant our flag on this hill. For every time they harden their hearts, firm up our resolve, and when they double down, give us a double portion of faith in our Lord Jesus Christ, who reigns with thee and our Father, one God, in glory everlasting. *Amen.*

FOR JUNETEENTH

O Spirit who leads captivity captive, making us the heralds of emancipation from slavery in all its myriad forms, we exult in thy deliverance which reached Galveston in 1865. Extend this tradition across our nation in breadth and depth. Liberate us from the injustice which continues unabolished, and enforce that reparation which has been proclaimed but not yet fully enforced. Show to us the jubilation of these forebears, a newfound mobility and self-determination, and the satisfying smell of barbecue which carries the memory of a people whose hope is stayed on Jesus Christ, who reigns with thee and our Father, one God, now and forever. *Amen.*

FOR FOOD JUSTICE

O Christ our daily bread, usher in a reality of food sovereignty. Uproot our systems of stolen land, exploited labor, and food apartheid. Give us healthy, culturally appropriate food and sustainable methods. Decenter corporations and the rich; put those who produce, distribute, and consume food, especially Black and Indigenous folk, at the heart of food systems. Redistribute land, protect farmworkers' rights, foster mutual aid, give us ecological humility, and provide universal access, that we might taste and see that thou art good, reigning with the Father and the Holy Spirit, one God, now and forever. *Amen.*

FOR NON-BLACK POC FIGHTING ANTI-BLACK RACISM WITHIN THEIR COMMUNITIES

O Christ, who took a motley mix of minoritized peoples and made them a priestly kingdom over against earthly empire, strengthen those who are fighting anti-Blackness within their own minoritized communities. Save us from the zero-sum mindset which compounds the scarcity that whiteness creates; show us how our flourishing is mutually dependent and reinforcing. When it feels like we're fighting on multiple fronts, give us grace and rest, yet also resolve to trust that our every transfusion into Black veins restores the life of the whole body, whose heart is the Holy Spirit, who reigns with thee and our Father, one God, now and forever. *Amen.*

FOR MOURNING THE DEATH OF A LEGEND

O Spirit our helpmeet, who anoints some to lift up myriads, we gasp for the air that has been sucked out of our lungs. We grasp for thy hand even as it takes this bedrock, [name], out from under our feet. Make their countenance an icon which advances our insight into thy story-weaving, and their legacy a force that continues to expand our imagination, self-love, and power, through Jesus Christ the firstborn of all who transcend death, who reigns with thee and our Father, one God, now and forever. *Amen.*

FOR WHEN THE LORD SECURES THE BAG

O God whose way out of no way is always higher than our ways, we are shook. When we thought thou wast sleeping, in truth it was we who were sleeping on thee, unable to smell what thou wast cooking and entirely unprepared emotionally for thy surprise reveal. Thou art the player-coach who hit the devil with a hesi, put our hindrances on skates, and hit the buzzer-beater for us, and over here on the bench we are screaming and fainting. So, to the Father of miracles, script flips, and plot twists, who reigns with Jesus Christ our dark horse and the Holy Spirit, one God, be honor and glory, blessing and power, now and forever. *Amen.*

VI

WORK AND
VOCATION

I HAVE JUST recently become gainfully employed for the first time in my life. Between college, a fellowship program, and seminary, I'd only ever held part-time jobs—at the library, in the admissions office, as the worship intern, youth intern, pastoral care intern, etc. So I'm learning how to work full-time not only in a nontypical, not-9-to-5 setting, but also during a pandemic.

A daily self-examination that I've landed on in the past couple of months is, "Did I give God my faithful act of service today?" After every Bible study, youth group, confirmation class, or one-on-one, it is so tempting to evaluate the success of the meeting by attendance, or enthusiasm, or my own reaction to the discussion. But while I of course have an important part in those outcomes, I don't control or ensure or deliver them. Thinking and living as if I do is only going to lead me to conclude that I am awful at my job, that I am stealing from my employers and place of employment by not doing well enough, and, most gravely, that I am hindering the spiritual formation of the youths that have been entrusted to me.

It's been a slow shift, but I am gradually coming around to basing my self-evaluation on the good faith effort that I put into planning and executing our activities—not letting my mind go too far down the path of what I could have done to create a different outcome, but rather directing my thoughts toward the manner in which I organized and presented my loaves and fish to Jesus for him to then do with what he would do.

I hope that these collects can highlight and inform the manner of your faithfulness to the work God has given you to do.

FOR BEFORE AN INTERVIEW

O God, who alone is omniscient so as to truly answer the question "How would your friends describe you?," give us the words by which we may present ourselves as holistically and winsomely as possible. Make our résumés rise to the top of the stack like the prayers of the saints to thy holy of holies. Calm our nerves, give us confidence, and help us to connect in a genuine way, through Jesus Christ who by the Holy Spirit employs us in the work of the Father, one God, now and forever. *Amen.*

FOR BEFORE PRESENTING

O Father who unceasingly puts thine ongoing work on display, we entrust to thee all who will soon be performing or presenting. Give us clarity of expression, that we might connect with the minds and hearts of our audience. Channel any nervousness into excitement for the moment and for the opportunity. Give us confidence in our craft and grace for our mistakes. If there are other presenters, free us to give them our full attention and support. And as our work is magnified, let thy voice be amplified in us and through us, by the compelling utterance of the Holy Spirit, who reigns with thee and our Lord Jesus Christ, one God, now and forever. *Amen.*

FOR MENTAL HEALTH PROFESSIONALS

O Spirit whose providence extends from the celestial mysteries to the unsearched ocean depths to the enigmatic operations of our minds, equip mental health professionals to uncover and unpack the psyches of those whom they serve. Through their steady attentiveness make important neurological and psychosocial realities apparent, and give them the words with which to foster clarity and coherence. And extend their bandwidth to attend to their own self-care and well-being, as our Lord Jesus Christ often withdrew to pray, who reigns with thee and our Father, one God, now and forever. *Amen.*

FOR A STRIKE

O God who sends the rich away empty, who forbids the employer to withhold from the worker, govern this strike. Blaze a path for the gathering of strength in numbers, and the winning of adequate compensation, benefits, and protections. Uproot the deep-seated evil which sacrifices people on the altar of profit, and the vulnerability which produces strikebreakers. Bring us to a milieu of equity in which excessive wealth is eschewed and redistributed. And make this picket line impenetrable by the unitive ministry of the Holy Spirit, who reigns with our Father and our Lord Jesus Christ, one God, now and forever. *Amen.*

FOR ESSENTIAL WORKERS

O Christ, who took our vulnerability onto thyself, send thine angelic hosts to protect, preserve, and empower those whose ongoing work during crisis puts them in harm's way. Bless them for relieving our burdens, and help us, especially policymakers, to do all we can to relieve theirs, not least by commensurate compensation, vocal appreciation, and structural change which far outlasts this time of crisis. Though they routinely enter the fire, let not a hair of their heads be touched, and keep all but love and health from entering their homes, by the encompassment of the Holy Spirit, who reigns with thee and our Father, one God, unassailable. *Amen.*

FOR SCREEN FATIGUE

O Father whose eyes move to and fro throughout the earth to show thyself strong on our behalf, give us respite when our eyes grow tired of being stuck on our screens. When our heads hurt from time spent in video meetings, online classes, and all manner of digital work, give us respite in the form of natural light, embodied activity, and good sleep. Protect the health of our eyes and brains, and make possible for us a different balance, that we might partake of screens in a way that gives rather than drains life, by the energizing power of the Holy Spirit, who reigns with thee and our Lord Jesus Christ, one God, now and forever. *Amen.*

FOR AFTER LOSING ONE'S JOB

O God who makes a way in the wilderness and rivers in the desert, lift up the heads of those who have recently been laid off or have otherwise lost their livelihoods. Rebuke the Accuser and all lies of self-blame, inadequacy, undependability, and undesirability which might steal into their minds. Make a safety net out of friends, family, and community. Empower departments of labor to provide speedy assistance. Give them energy to get back up, and employ them again soon, for the sake of our Lord Jesus Christ for whom we work, who reigns with the Father and the Holy Spirit, one God, now and forever. *Amen.*

FOR SMALL BUSINESSES

O God of Lydia the merchant, Priscilla the tentmaker, and Peter the fisherman, we pray thy blessing upon small businesses. Give their owners the capital, strategy, publicity, and team they need to thrive. Help us to prioritize them in our consumption and political action. Use their services and products to solve problems and meet felt needs, and let them contribute to the culture and pride of their communities. In setbacks, protect and revive their dreams. And govern our economic lives in the positive-sum game of the kingdom of our Lord Jesus Christ, who reigns with the Father and the Holy Spirit, one God, now and forever. *Amen.*

FOR AFTER GETTING THE JOB OR OFFER

O God who celebrates us constantly, we ascribe all praise, honor, and power to thee for this offer of admission or employment. The experiences which comprise our résumés, the words with which we filled our applications, our perseverance through rejections, and the deliberations of hiring personnel were all guided by thy loving and mighty providence. Help us to savor this validation, prepare us for this transition, and party with us tonight as we toast to the Lord of Hosts, who reigns—Father, Son, and Holy Spirit—one God, now and forever. *Amen.*

FOR THE START OF A NEW JOB

O God whose hand turns the page and whose pen begins each new chapter, go before us into this new work. In thy good timing reveal all the ways in which it may contribute to the coming of thy kingdom, and sustain us through the ways in which it is distorted by opposing powers. Enrich our relationships with coworkers and supervisors. Make our mistakes instructive, our questions generative, and our contributions effective as we work as unto our Lord Jesus Christ, who reigns with thee and the Holy Spirit, one God, working all things unto glory. *Amen.*

FOR EDUCATORS

O Wonderful Counselor, we commend unto thee all educators. Bless them one hundredfold for their heart and commitment to empowering young people. For every late night and early morning spent lesson-planning, grading, or going the extra mile, restore unto them time and rest. Make students intellectually curious and respectful. Make parents cooperative, and administration supportive. Bring about the political change whereby they might be much better compensated. And lead us into deeper knowledge of ourselves, our world, and our Lord Jesus Christ, who reigns with our Father and the Holy Spirit, one God, in wisdom everlasting. *Amen.*

FOR BEFORE A BIG TEST

O Christ, who as a youth showed thyself learned in the wisdom valued by thy people, whose abilities of creative reasoning and rhetoric were later constantly put to the test, we pray for those taking standardized or comprehensive exams. Give them calm and clarity of recall. Enable them to showcase the breadth and depth of their preparation. And though this moment looms large now, help them to zoom out and see that what ultimately defines their value and trajectory is not this exam, but rather the providence of our Father, who reigns with thee and the Holy Spirit, one God, now and forever. *Amen.*

FOR WHEN ONE DREADS THE THOUGHT OF RETURNING TO WORK ON MONDAY

O Christ, conqueror over the trying and lord of the mundane, we commend this upcoming workweek to thee. When our tasks are monotonous, unfulfilling, or draining, kindly show us moments of meaning. When our coworkers are difficult to be with, bring remedy to those relationships. Guide both our making the most of our current situation and our dreams of better employment, as thou hast taught us to do in all respects while we live in a broken world and yet anticipate the consummation of the kingdom of our Lord Jesus Christ, who reigns with thee and our Father, one God, now and forever. *Amen.*

FOR FOCUS

O Father, singularly focused in thy ministry and providence, we beseech thee for the soundness of mind ascribed to us in thy holy Scriptures. Through tweets, grams, and other distractions, tune our minds to the frequency of thy stillness. Let us rely on thine empowerment rather than on the adrenaline which attends an imminent deadline. And make us to eschew the instant gratification of diversion in favor of a deeper payoff, that we might hear thy Spirit say to our hearts, "Well done, good and faithful servant," to thy parental pride and the honor of our Lord Jesus Christ, one God, now and forever. *Amen.*

FOR BEFORE ENTERING A MEETING THAT COULD'VE BEEN AN EMAIL

O Christ, patient yet firm with those who sought an audience with thee for ill-considered reasons, give us thy composure as we enter this meeting that could have and should have been an email. Graciously salvage some modicum of team-building or helpful discussion here. Yet also kindly make the inefficiency of this session so apparent that all, especially our supervisors, determine to operate differently in the future. Redeem this time, as thou art able to redeem all that is lost, O Lord Jesus Christ, who lives and reigns with the Father and the Holy Spirit, one God, now and forever. *Amen.*

FOR THOSE WHO HAVE DIFFICULT SUPERVISORS

O Christ, long-suffering for our sake in the face of mistreatment from authorities, we ask thee to bear up those who have difficult relationships with supervisors. When we express our concerns, make them receptive and willing to adjust. If they double down on their ways, give us a divine forbearance. Give us friends with whom to vent, moments of respite, and if it be thy will, a change in personnel, that our work relationships may be more conducive to our doing the work thou hast given us to do for thy kingdom, where thou dost reign with the Father and the Holy Spirit, one God, in harmony everlasting. *Amen.*

FOR TECHNICAL DIFFICULTIES

O God our Creator and Lord of all we in turn have created, we request thine intervention in this moment of technological frustration. As thou hast moved upon the most intricate operations of our bodies, minds, and souls, kindly place thy remedial hand upon this [printer, sound system, server, etc.]. Restore it to proper functioning, that we might progress with the work thou hast given us to do. Though all we fashion be subject to entropy and futility, we appeal to the ever-effective, ever-fruitful reality of the inbreaking kingdom of our Lord Jesus Christ, who reigns with thee and the Holy Spirit, one God, now and forever. *Amen.*

FOR ORGANIZERS AND ACTIVISTS

O God of Rosa, Fannie, and Coretta, we commend to thee all organizers and activists. Champion those who envision and pursue a just society. Anoint them with a double portion of the spirit of the prophets whose mantle they wear. Sustain the clarity of their vision, the power of their communities, their resources, and the longevity of their political and structural accomplishments. Give them courage to speak truth to power, endurance for the struggle, and space for rest and self-care. And make their work a foretaste of the kingdom of our Lord Jesus Christ, who reigns with our Mother and the Holy Spirit, one God, world without end. *Amen.*

FOR WHEN ONE'S WORK IS UNDERAPPRECIATED

O Christ, custodian of our fulfilled and our dashed hopes, soothe our hearts. Thou art well acquainted with the feeling of receiving an underwhelming or even dissenting reaction to thy work and thy heart which thou didst and dost offer on our behalf. So when our offerings are received poorly, or evaluated harshly, fortify us. Make us content with what we did well. Make criticism serve constructive ends, that we may know where and how to improve. And orient us to the system of honor and approval of which the only arbiter is our Father, who reigns with thee and the Holy Spirit, one God, now and forever. *Amen.*

FOR THOSE WORKING IN RETAIL

O attendant Christ, who gave thirty years to a workaday trade, we ask for thy grace upon all those working in retail. We commend them to thy endurance for the long shifts and thy patience for dealing with unkind customers. Make their managers calm and considerate, particularly in times of crisis or stress. Bless them with wholesome interactions with lovely people, as well as with increasingly adequate compensation. And as they provide for our wants and needs, do form them into the likeness of the Father whose provision is made perfect through Jesus Christ our Lord, by the gift of the Holy Spirit, one God, now and forever. *Amen.*

FOR ANTI-RACISM EDUCATION

O Christ the Word, who judges the thoughts and attitudes of the heart, make all anti-racist educators like hands guiding the sword which divides soul from spirit, intention from impact, and interpersonal reality from structural complicity. Make their students committed to the process of transformation. Compensate them financially and emotionally for the unique toll that this work exacts. Make every lecture given, resource offered, discussion facilitated, and action item recommended an advance against the powers of darkness, who tremble at the name of Jesus Christ who reigns with our Father and the Holy Spirit, one God, now and forever. *Amen.*

FOR GRADUATING SENIORS

O God who orders our steps, we lift up those who are finishing high school and moving on to new chapters of their vocational lives. As they enter the workforce or further education, assure them of thine ongoing providence, and remind them of thy past provision. When that which previously defined them is stripped away, guide their construction of a fuller identity and worldview. Meet them out at the boundaries they push, and inside in the questions they ask. Weave their old and new communities together, and in uncharted seas let their anchor be our Lord Jesus Christ, who reigns with thee and the Holy Spirit, one God, now and forever. *Amen.*

FOR WHEN SOMEONE IS CRUSHING IT MORE THAN YOU ARE

O God who crafts, names, and gifts each of us with treasure from a boundless trove, we thank thee for the unique talents, skills, and opportunities thou hast provided us. When our giftings or aspirations overlap with those of others, help us reject mindsets of competition and scarcity, that we might instead appraise the positive sum of the spaces, resources, and connections we collectively create as we stake our hope on the ongoing overabundance of our Lord Jesus Christ, who reigns with thee and the Holy Spirit, one God, now and forever. *Amen.*

FOR VIRTUAL LEARNING

O God by whom we have access to knowledge and wonder, enable us to glean as much as we can from virtual education. As we feel the loss of the in-between and extracurricular moments that fill out our learning experience, show us new sparks of curiosity, delight, and connection. Breathe motivation into us, form receptiveness in us, empower us to take ownership of what we study. Give us margin in uncharted territory, grace for each other, and cooperative tech as we seek to resource one another by the provision of the Holy Spirit our Teacher, who reigns with thee and our Lord Jesus Christ, one God, now and forever. *Amen.*

FOR CREATIVE WORK

O Holy Maker, who brings order and beauty out of chaos, ignite a spark of creativity in our hearts, minds, and bodies as we seek to make something out of nothing. Spirit, let the breath of thy inspiration touch us, fill us, and move us. Govern our trial and error, our stabs in the dark, our striking out into the void, and the slow crystallization of our ideas. Let what we create be accessible and enlightening to others, and glorifying to thee. We thank thee for making us co-creators with thee and our Father and our Lord Jesus Christ, one God, world without end. *Amen.*

VII

RECREATION

IN MY THEOLOGICAL imagination, the new earth is where all of our activity becomes recreation. We may very well continue to do many of the things that we knew as work on the old earth, but because they are now being done in an environment where the presence of God is full in extent and degree, and all futility has been done away with and replaced with glorious, immediate meaning and beauty and goodness, it is better thought of as recreation because it is part of our neverending *re-creation*, our "further up and further in" to God's perfectly restful life.

In the same way a single word can change a feeling of anxiety into a prayer, and a simple acknowledgment of God can turn despair into holy lament, I believe a single word or simple prayer can transform that which could be merely amusement into holy re-creation. Even when you're watching trash TV, or scrolling through social media, or making memes in order to relate to the youths. That's what the collects in this section represent—a way of formalizing our knowledge that wherever there is true delight, there is an opportunity to enjoy God; to make that happiness into a prism refracting our primary and ultimate delight in God (and God's in us).

Another implication of this eschatology is that not only does God have a sense of humor, but humor, insofar as it is one of our most powerful "idioms of delight," is actually part and parcel of the beatitude for which we were created, and for which we were and are re-created now and for eternity.

God is the supreme observational humorist. For every connection I see that leads to "real housewife of Christ" and our tithes being "JC's penny," God sees a million more, and, I do believe, finds joy in them and encourages us to use them as ways to explore the interconnectedness of God's creation and the permeation of all good things by God's presence.

Over the course of writing this collection, I've also seen how effective humor is as a rhetorical device. Bringing into prayer the parts of our brains and hearts that uniquely respond to humor creates potential for internalization, memorization, and, more broadly, deeper reception of the devotional significance of the prayer.

So let's bring our playfulness, our wit, and our whimsy to God just as we bring our adoration, confession, thanksgiving, and supplication. And let's bring all the things we do just for the sheer pleasure of them, as a foretaste of the time in which the unmitigated pleasure of God will imbue all that we do.

And thus are those who have stood by God who glorified them, they persevere, astounded by the excess of glory, and by the endless addition of divinity's splendor. For the end will be eternal progress, the condition of additional, endless fulfillment, and shall make an attainment of the Unattainable, and God of whom no one can get enough, shall become the source of satisfaction for all.

But the full measure of Him and the glory of His light will be an abyss of progress, and an endless beginning . . . runners do not overtake the end of the infinite . . . and so those who have a share in Him, those who dwell in Him, how may they embrace all of Him, and so be satisfied?

How, tell me, would they grasp the end of the endless? It is impossible and by all means impracticable. For thus neither in the saints still in the body, nor for those departed to God, can such a thought at all penetrate them . . . they truly know as though by every certainty that their perfection shall be endless, and the progress shall be everlasting.*

—Saint Symeon the New Theologian

* Taken from Gheorghe Ovidiu Sferlea, "On the Interpretation of the Theory of Perpetual Progress (*Epektasis*): Taking into Account the Testimony of Eastern Monastic Tradition," July 2014, *Revue d'histoire Ecclésiastique* 109 (3-4): 564–87.

FOR BEFORE HITTING THE DANCE FLOOR

O Lord of boundless delight, whom the psalmist instructs us to praise with the dance, who animates and sets in motion all the beauty of our world, wouldst thou enliven our bodies now. Do so move upon this disc jockey to supply a steady stream of bangers, as well as a satisfying balance of hits and deep tracks, oldies and contemporaries, salsa and bachata, and even those jams for which we know not to ask. We ask for magical moments with cuties, whimsical use of booties, and for there to be enough soul in the room for a *Soul Train* line to be possible. We ask all this that we may now anticipate the wedding feast of the Lamb, where we will dance with our Bridegroom, our Lord Jesus Christ, who reigns with thee and the Holy Spirit, one God, now and forever. *Amen.*

FOR BEFORE WATCHING A ROM-COM

O Christ our soulmate, create unlikely sustenance once again by making this rom-com into nom-noms which nourish our sentimental souls. Deliver us from the folly of full-grown actors playing teens, magic and spark as substitute for hard work, and the guy whose hotness earns him way too many chances. For thou art the best of the bad boi and the nice guy; subversive yet conscientious, lofty yet accessible, mysterious yet available, exciting yet dependable, bird of our feather yet radically other. So from all the boys thou hast loved before, and the girls next door to thy heavenly courts, be worship to thee and our Father and the Holy Spirit, one God, divine romance. *Amen.*

FOR BEFORE WATCHING TRASH TV

O Spirit whose deep investment in our lives we do not deserve, turn this trash into compost which by thy mysterious and miraculous working enriches our lives. As our enjoyment moves along the ironic-genuine continuum, use this show to make us feel better about our lives, our emotional intelligence, and our conflict-resolution skills. For thou art the producer who edits our lives to maximize not drama but rather peace and wholeness. And while we stan certain persons, thou art the one who champions us and makes us, the church, the real housewife of Christ, who reigns with thee and our Father, one God, now and forever. *Amen.*

FOR BEFORE JOURNALING

O Christ the Word sent and made known to us, help us to put our thoughts down on the page. Make this a release valve for the buildup of our deepest feelings, and channel this into a flow which carries us toward connections, breakthroughs, and self-awareness. Help us to concretize thoughts that can otherwise remain too abstract or unmoored to be helpful. Deliver unto us the value of being able to go back and see what we were thinking in the past, and ultimately direct our mindfulness toward the One who is always mindful of us— our Father, who reigns with thee and the Holy Spirit, one God, now and forever. *Amen.*

FOR BEFORE PLAYING ULTIMATE

O Spirit whose breath is the wind that refreshes our souls and carries our discs, look at the flick of our wrists and the exhilaration in our hearts as we play. When we line up to throw off, whether we yell "ultimate," "coming in," or "for Narnia," be the ultimate grace which comes into our souls and allows us to enjoy thee in all manner of play and playfulness. Make our throws precise as thy providence over creation, our layouts like thine outstretched arms of love, and our give-and-go like our reception and advancement of the gospel of our Lord Jesus Christ, who reigns with thee and our Father, one God, now and forever. *Amen.*

FOR BEFORE OPENING UP BUZZFEED

O omniscient God, who needs no quiz to know which Disney princess we truly are, it is thou who works through our study of popular culture to help us love ourselves, our neighbors, our world, and (reason #4 has blown our minds) thyself. Thus, as we peruse celebrity goings-on, hot lewks, and tweet and TikTok roundups, entertain and enlighten us. For thy companionship is more inconceivable and delightful than an unlikely animal friendship, thy commandments are the foremost listicle, and thy redemption of humanity is the DIY project of our Lord Jesus Christ, who reigns with the Father and the Holy Spirit, one God, in glory everlasting. *Amen.*

FOR VEGGIETALES KIDS

O God who is bigger than the boogeyman, who loves us more than King George loves his duckies, more than Larry loves Barbara Manatee, thou hast helped us to find not only our hairbrush but also our reason to live. Though we had gotten ourselves into a giant pickle, like Larryboy thou didst swoop in to save us. Therefore let us not be pirates who don't do anything but rather use this produce to produce holiness in us, and bring us to that day in which everyone indeed has a water buffalo, that glorious day of our Lord Jesus Christ, who reigns with our Father and the Holy Spirit, one God, now and forever. *Amen.*

FOR BEFORE WALKING INTO THE MALL

O Father who delivers us from the temple of consumerism into thy holy sanctuary, preserve us as we enter this mall. Though the ads aim to twist and turn our desires like one of Auntie Anne's pretzels, let thy grace be the escalator which transports our thoughts upward to the truly hot topics of thy revealed wisdom. For thine altar is the true genius bar, our tithes the true JC's penny, and thy parousia the truly victorious secret. So bring us to that heavenly banquet, the food court prepared for us by the One who baptized us in the old navy waters—our Lord Jesus Christ, who reigns with thee and the Holy Spirit, one God, now and forever. *Amen.*

FOR SELECTING A NEW SHOW TO WATCH

O Spirit whose revelation provides profound entertainment, we beseech thee now for courage to leave the security blanket of [go-to show] and venture out into the unknown realms of the streaming universe. Whether we be escapists or realists, comedy- or drama-lovers, bring to us—through friends' recommendation or Buzzfeed listicle—a program with the writing and acting prowess of *This Is Us,* the casting magic of *New Girl,* and the catharsis of *Queer Eye.* And let us become enraptured yet always binge first and foremost the narratives breathed by our Lord Jesus Christ, who reigns with thee and our Father, one God, world without end. *Amen.*

FOR DISNEY CHANNEL KIDS

O God who adopts us into thy proud family, we praise thee for the suite life thou hast given and sustained in us. Like Raven, give us foretastes of the mysterious and glorious future thou hast for us, yet nevertheless help us also to get our heads in the game right now. And whether we be cheetah girls or boyz 'n motion, help us to strut down the straight and narrow path like we mean it, and give thee our devotion. Now to the One who does the kimpossible—who gives us the best of both worlds, this and the next—Father, Son, and Holy Spirit—be honor and blessing, now and forever. *Amen.*

FOR PIXAR FANS

O God who reigns to infinity and beyond, we praise thee. Thou art the one who brought us back from the land of the dead and awakened us with the sweet songs of salvation. Thou hast crossed land and ocean to find and rescue us. Thou hast turned our screams into laughter, giving us courage for the adventure that is out there. So make the armor of God our super suit, transform us from the inside out, and at the last bring us, like Wall-E, from this dying world into thy new world, and install us there as kings and mcqueens, to the glory of our Lord Jesus Christ, who reigns with the Father and the Holy Spirit, one God, now and forever. *Amen.*

FOR BEFORE EATING KRISPY KREME

O Spirit whose mercies are fresher than a glazed cascading down under the light of the HOT sign, make us like that donut—hot and holy—on fire for the gospel and set apart as is Krispy Kreme from all competitors. Sprinkle us with thine anointing, give us a sweet inner filling of peace, and make us always leave room at our core for thy lordship. And as twelve is a number of perfection in thy Scriptures, may we receive thy favor to go ahead and order a dozen, whether to eat alone or to share at church, enriching our worship of our Lord Jesus Christ, who reigns with thee and our Father, one God, in glory everlasting. *Amen.*

FOR WHEN ONE'S TEAM IS STRUGGLING

O Spirit of consolation, we come to lament that our team is struggling this year. When L's are all we have to hold, wouldst thou take our burdens upon thyself. May we viscerally remember our former glory, and hope in thy governance over our collective future. In staying the course may we grow into the likeness of the one who is no fair-weather fan of us, the coach who put us in, whom we love to play for—our Father, who reigns with thee and our Lord Jesus Christ, one God, in dynasty unending. *Amen.*

FOR A SERIES FINALE

O God who resolves and subsumes all good storylines in thine unending narrative, we pray thy providence over this series finale. We lament the end of a good thing—comfort us, and help us reach the day in which nothing we love will leave. Let the inspiration and blessing thou hast given us through this show continue to bear fruit in our lives. And whether these characters ride off into the sunset, or stop each other's planes, or fall back in love, or realize their dreams, we simply ask that this finale avoid all semblance of that of *How I Met Your Mother,* by the grace of our Father and the Lord Jesus Christ and the Holy Spirit, one God, world without end. *Amen.*

FOR UNITY AMONGST STAR WARS FANS

O Christ, whose death and resurrection retconned all of human existence, we pray thee for unity amongst we who stan.

Like the church at Corinth, each of us says, "I belong to Rian Johnson," or "I belong to J. J. Abrams," or "I belong to George Lucas." So make our different allegiances, fan theories, and hermeneutics a source of harmony, revealing ultimately the way we have all been formed and delighted by these narratives. And as thou hast done with *Rogue One* and most exquisitely with Baby Yoda, continue to sow consensus in unexpected ways, by the unitive ministry of the Holy Spirit, who reigns with thee and our Father, one God, world without end. *Amen.*

FOR BEFORE AN ONLINE HUMBLEBRAG

O God, who incorporates us into thy triumph, we come to humble ourselves prior to sharing big news online. We are grateful for what thou hast done in us, and the friends thou hast given us to share it with. But we recognize that this news might cause a twinge of sadness, regret, or longing in others—make us sensitive to all such possibility, and show us the best way to show love to them now, perhaps even by a personal note. Spirit, examine us and remove from us all pride and self-centering, that our news might ultimately point to the good news of the gospel of our Lord Jesus Christ, who reigns with thee and the Father, one God, now and forever. *Amen.*

FOR BEFORE HITTING THE GYM

O God our strong tower, creator of bodies capable of amazing things, we request thy presence as we enter the gym. Make our workout regimen like our spiritual disciplines—consistent in repetition, effective in formation. Whether we seek strength, balance, flexibility, or stamina, give us the endurance of Paul, the moxie of Esther, and the dedication of Ruth. Make each lunge, squat, press, pull, and lift an act of bodily stewardship, and a means of grace, that our souls may be made swole by our Lord Jesus Christ, who reigns with thee and the Holy Spirit, one God, now and forever. *Amen.*

FOR BEFORE CRACKING OPEN A GOOD BOOK

O Lord who creates worlds with words, show to us once again the wonder of absorption in a work of literature. Let us lose ourselves in it, and find ourselves in it. Let it jump-start our imagination and curiosity and hunger for the good, true, and beautiful. Let it orient us toward, and embed us in, thine overarching narrative. Whether it be a page-turner or more of the "read one page and our head explodes" variety, make it a boon to our souls, that we may be reminded of the perfect and supreme authorship of our Lord Jesus Christ, who writes with the Father and the Holy Spirit, one God, story without end. *Amen.*

FOR BEFORE HOOPING

O Lord of the loaves, fishes, and swishes—we do love to enter thy courts, not least this hardwood. We entreat thee now to multiply our assist-to-turnover ratio as thou didst multiply sustenance for the crowd. Help us to go as hard in the paint as thou didst go in the temple turning tables, yet make our finger roll as gentle as the sea thou didst still. Make our bodies and our hearts limber to resolve conflict. Father, make our shooting motion as consistent as thy grace, and allow us to cross over our defenders as swiftly as thou didst make us cross over from death to the life of our Lord Jesus Christ, who reigns with thee and the Holy Spirit, one God, dynasty without end. *Amen.*

FOR BEFORE WALKING INTO TARGET

O Jehovah Jireh, who satisfies our souls and makes our hearts content, we beseech thee for a spirit of moderation as we walk into Target. Though the ambience, wide aisles, and $1.00 section be prone to suck us in, let thy guiding hand keep us on mission. When our cart overflows, help us to separate the wheat from the chaff. When sales and bargains compel us, help us to hear the voice of our bank account crying out for mercy. And may this department store remind us of thy provision for every department of our lives, O Father, reigning with our Lord Jesus Christ and the Holy Spirit, one God, now and forever. *Amen.*

VIII

MUSIC

I, LIKE MANY people, spend a big portion of my waking hours listening to music. Outside of religious texts, song lyrics make up the majority of the words that are most deeply embedded in my soul. When I had the idea to compile several of my favorite song titles and turns of phrase from The Oh Hellos into a collect, I was conveniently sitting in a lovely seminary courtyard in New York City, taking in a picturesque morning. Reflecting on the various connections between the already-very-profound Oh Hellos lyrics was a sweet spiritual exercise; a way of drawing out the theological and devotional significance of the individual songs, the albums, and the discography as a whole.

I later enjoyed the challenge of doing similar liturgical work on less immediately sacred music, digging into the mix of '70s funk, '00s CCM, and '10s indie music from a variety of genres that makes up my library.

Perhaps you'll recognize some of these artists. Consider the ones you don't my recommendations for you. And consider this chapter an invitation to create God-talk out of the song titles and lyrics that mean the most to you.

FOR AFTER DISCOVERING A NEW BAND OR ARTIST

O Spirit whose joy it is to surprise us, there is no blessing quite like the wonder, delight, and fulfillment of discovering new music which we love. Like stumbling upon a beautiful landscape, or making a new best friend, it is like becoming a child again. Let the notes lift our souls, the lyrics lift our minds, and the time spent listening be a deep Sabbath rest. And whether we seek to hold on to the special feeling of sole ownership over hidden treasure, or to bring others into our discovery, make this music a prism which refracts the light of the glory of our Lord Jesus Christ, who reigns with thee and our Father, one God, in unending song. *Amen.*

FOR WHEN A SONG IS STUCK IN ONE'S HEAD

O Christ, who shepherds us through wormwood and earworm alike, deliver us when our minds function like broken records. Save our brain cells from the untimely death which results from our inadvertent fixation and endless repetition of the one line we know. Let not the inane lyrics and catchy melodies be embedded in our long-term memory, but rather reveal to us the perfect song with which to overrun, replace, and eject the object of our torment, as thou dost accomplish spiritually in our hearts by the lordship of the Holy Spirit, who reigns with thee and our Father, one God, now and forever. *Amen.*

FOR A BAND BREAKUP

O Christ our lifelong collaborator, we lament the end of an era. Upon losing the inspiration of our muse, the anticipation of what they might do next, and the possibility of seeing them live, our hearts are heavy. Whether this be due to creative differences, financial difficulty, personal conflict, or gig weariness, give them the rest and space they need, and maintain always a glimmer of hope for a reunion. And continue to give this music life which far transcends its creators, by the mysteries of the Holy Spirit, who reigns with thee and our Father, one God, now and forever. *Amen.*

FOR NOSTALGIC MUSIC

O Holy Spirit whose being extends across time, transport us through this music to the days and years for which it is the soundtrack. Draw out even the most abstract and vague memories and feelings that these notes evoke, that we might connect with our past selves and past lives, gaining momentary transcendence and lasting perspective. And bring us to the day in which thy presence restores to us goodness long past, out of the storehouses of our Father, who reigns with thee and our Lord Jesus Christ, one God, now and forever. *Amen.*

FOR BEFORE LISTENING TO JOSH GARRELS

O Friend who sticks closer than a brother, who crossed the sea in between to be our rescue from floodwaters and our hiding place, we rejoice in being the colors thou hast unwound and woven into a wave of beautiful sound. As such, make us bring glory to the Light which came down when our time had come to be born again. And as by the light of the moon we press on, guide us farther along until we hear thee say, "Peace to all who enter here," and receive the Shepherd's song, the benediction of our Lord Jesus Christ, who reigns with our Father and the Holy Spirit, one God, now and forever. *Amen.*

FOR BEFORE LISTENING TO JUMP5

O Christ, who for the joyride set before you endured the cross, it's like we have nothing to do but think about you, for you have given us all the time in the world to do just that. And though sometimes we wish that we could read your mind, we know that you have empowered us to change a heart and thereby change the world. So to you, and to the Holy Spirit who makes us living stones and rocks this spiritual house all the way down, and to our Father in whose arms we are spinning around—one God—be dominion and splendor, now and forever. *Amen.*

FOR BEFORE LISTENING TO LIONEL RICHIE

O Christ, with whom we ascend until we are dancing on the ceiling, hello—it truly was thee we were looking for. We know ourselves to be wandering strangers in this world, but with every step we're coming home to thee. Make us like deep river women, letting the current of thy grace wash over us, for thou art our endless love—we'll say it for always; that's the way it should be. So let thy music play on, and let thy people dance all night long with thee who reigns with our Father and the Holy Spirit, one God, world without end. *Amen.*

FOR BEFORE LISTENING TO HAWK NELSON

O Christ, who surpasses every little thing we've wanted, we praise thee for thine ability to wield good out of all the things we go through. We tried to be perfect, tried to be honest, but thou hast always wanted us simply because we are thine own. That calling is often a long and lonely road, but even when thou art the one thing we have left, we have enough. So whether we need one little miracle, or simply have a lot of things we want to say, give us a chance to find a way. And bring us to that unending day where the sunshine takes us there to the Father of lights, who reigns with thee and the Holy Spirit, one God, world without end. *Amen.*

FOR BEFORE LISTENING TO SNARKY PUPPY

O Spirit who tore the curtain and awoke every sleeper, thou hast freed our dreams and brought us into the clearing, the open and spacious place of abundant life, and we like it here. We had gone under, deep into the flood, but thy grace rescued us and opened our mouths to say to the devil, "I'm not the one." And now as thy disciples we are outliers in this world, but we thereby have something in common with thy beloved community, which is a thing of gold. So on thy wings give us flight and continue to bring us the bright until we reach that unending family dinner hosted by thee and our Father and our Lord Jesus Christ, one God, in glory everlasting. *Amen*.

FOR BEFORE LISTENING TO THE COMMODORES

O Spirit by whose winds we sail on through the seas of life, thou art a more sure foundation than a brick house. Whether we be easy like Sunday morning, or pushing through the nightshift, let us hear thy sweet sounds coming down, and thy voice saying, "Wake up children, won't ye come dance with me?" Heaven knows it is thou who brings us up when we're down and changes our life around such that we feel too hot to trot. And by creation, redemption, and consummation we are three times a lady—the bride of our Lord Jesus Christ, who reigns with thee and our Father, one God, now and forever. *Amen*.

FOR BEFORE LISTENING TO NEWSBOYS

O Spirit in whom we are free to run, by thy grace wherever we go we are entertaining angels. Help us step up to the microphone and declare that God is not a secret, that the world might see good works and glorify the Lord. And until we reach that eternal love liberty disco, there will always be praises on our tongue from our heart for our God who became flesh—our Lord Jesus Christ, the name we are not ashamed to speak, the final answer to who we want our God to be—who reigns with thee and our Father, one God, now and forever. *Amen*.

FOR BEFORE LISTENING TO STEVIE WONDER

O Christ who signed, sealed, and delivered us unto the Father, we just call to say we love you. We are always dancing to the rhythm of your love, for we can feel it all over. Though we must believe in things we don't understand, your Spirit tells us "you will know," and that by faith, with fear and trembling, we can work it out. And although at times we reminisce and wish those days would come back once more, nevertheless we are living for the city—the New Jerusalem—and we will keep on trying 'til we reach the higher ground of our Lord Jesus Christ, who reigns with our Father and the Holy Spirit, one God, world without end. *Amen.*

FOR BEFORE LISTENING TO LAKE STREET DIVE

O Holy Spirit, who does not leave us alone with our thoughts but rather guards our hearts and minds with peace, thou hast wrought good out of godawful things to bring us right back to thee. When devils whispered "shame, shame, shame," thou didst command Satan to call off his dogs, that through thy power and grace we might free ourselves up. So help us to master ourselves, that we might no longer take bad self-portraits but rather come to recognize in ourselves the image of our Lover who will be back again another day—Jesus Christ who reigns with thee and our Father, one God, now and forever. *Amen.*

FOR BEFORE LISTENING TO FAMILY FORCE 5

O Christ, whose death shook us like an earthquake and whose resurrection causes us to forever put our hands up in praise, it is thou who looked upon the world and said, "Hold up, wait a minute, let me put a little love in it." Thou hast given us reason to get our backs off the wall—to declare a dance war on the devil. And now, whether we be kountry gentlemen or drama queens, we belong to the one who did the saving business up front and now hastens us unto the party in the back stretch of our existence—the eschaton of our Father, who reigns with thee and the Holy Spirit, one God, now and forever. *Amen.*

FOR BEFORE LISTENING TO THE ISLEY BROTHERS

O Spirit whose love is the harvest for the world, let your still, small voice be the summer breeze which cools us out. We seek nothing more than to groove with you—welcome into our hearts. You showed us how to follow your footsteps in the dark road to Calvary, that we might die with you and rise again to new life. And now we will hurry up and wait for your return, wherein you say you will win the showdown with death and the devil, securing glory and passing it on to us, those redeemed by our Lord Jesus Christ, who reigns with you and our Father, one God, world without end. *Amen.*

FOR BEFORE LISTENING TO MUTEMATH

O Christ, who broke the spell of the typical and made us odd souls, take control of our chaos. When our blood pressure rises, and when we are walking paranoia, return us to the monument of your love for us. When we are stalling out, or stranded in the stratosphere, and when our surefire plans have backfired again, tell our hearts "heads up" and remind us that we are still far from over. Nothing can stop what you started, nothing can break what you bonded, and we will always light up for you. Always forever we remain in our Father, who reigns with you and the Holy Spirit, one God, in glory everlasting. *Amen.*

FOR BEFORE LISTENING TO ALLEN STONE

O Spirit who assigns to us guardian angels, who loosed us from our sin that we might get lifted up by righteousness, we praise thee. When we are unaware of our failings, or when we must sleep in the bed we've made, help us to say, "I know that I wasn't right," that we might be restored and empowered to love where we're at. Save us from the callousness of American privilege, make us warriors against all powers of evil, and help us to be faithful until we reach that perfect world ruled by our Lord Jesus Christ, who reigns with thee and our Father, one God, world without end. *Amen.*

FOR BEFORE LISTENING TO AUDIO ADRENALINE

O Mighty Good Leader, who when we get down dost lift us up, thou hast removed our sins to the ocean floor and sent thy church worldwide to be thy hands and feet. Surely we are never going to be as big as Jesus, but if we keep our eyes on him we can walk on water, for by thy preserving hand we will not fade but rather join the hit parade of the one who brings all of us church punks and underdogs to that big house with lots and lots of room—the house prepared for us by our Lord Jesus Christ, who reigns with thee and the Holy Spirit, one God, now and forever. *Amen.*

FOR BEFORE LISTENING TO AVERAGE WHITE BAND

O Father who picked up the pieces of this broken world and made it new, we are grateful that you have given us work to do for your kingdom. For we were soul searching until we discovered that your love is a miracle. It enables us to have a love of our own, which we may share person-to-person. And though the world is cloudy now, we know that with every step we are goin' home, so let us never lose this heaven until we cut the cake at the great wedding reception of the Lamb, Jesus Christ, who reigns with thee and the Holy Spirit, one God, world without end. *Amen.*

FOR BEFORE LISTENING TO FRANKIE BEVERLY

O Christ, by whose redemption we are back in stride with God, we know thou canst tell by the look in our eyes that we are falling in love with thee. We were running away, and playing too many games, but thou hast brought us out of this maze into the golden time of day. It is thou who shepherds us through joy and pain, who keeps us in thy grip before we let go, who feels what we're feelin', who wants us to feel that we're wanted, and in whom we are one by the unitive ministry of the Holy Spirit, who reigns with thee and our Father, one God, now and forever. *Amen.*

FOR BEFORE LISTENING TO EARTH, WIND & FIRE

O God our devotion, our shining star, thou hast made us to sing a song. Thy love has found its way in our hearts tonight, keeping our heads to the sky, whence descends the land of our holy fantasy. When trouble be the way of the world, when evil be running through our brains, and when our reasons start to fade, help us to get away, and be once again to us the spice of life which makes us groove tonight, until we reach that boogie wonderland, dancing with Father, Son, and Holy Spirit, one God, in glory everlasting. *Amen.*

FOR EARLY '00S KIDS

O Spirit who fills the household of faith with love from the windows to the walls, we are crazy in love with thee, and consequently we seek to take our faith and walk it out. When the world is tearing up our hearts, and shaking us like a polaroid picture, remind us of the one-two step of thy justification and sanctification, by which we fly high—no lie. Thou art the gold digger who took us from the miry clay and refined us in fire, that we might not lose our minds up in here but rather be made truly fergalicious by our Lord Jesus Christ, who reigns with thee and our Father, one God, now and forever. *Amen.*

FOR BEFORE LISTENING TO TOBYMAC

O Father who got this party started, we dedicate these songs to every one of God's children. Thou hast given us a ticket to ride upon the J train, where thy redemptive momentum has had thy saints on a roll for two thousand years or so. In these extreme days, we seek not to gain the whole world and lose our souls, but rather to remember that we were made to love by the one who brings us to the diverse city of thy holy Zion, where love is in the house and the house is packed in honor of our Lord Jesus Christ, who reigns with thee and the Holy Spirit, one God, world without end. *Amen.*

FOR BEFORE LISTENING TO CHICAGO

O God of our beginnings, in whom we are alive again and feeling stronger every day, you're the inspiration. Our besetting sins are a hard habit to break, and it's hard for us to say we're sorry, but with love you say, "Call on me," and with forgiveness you make us smile. You made our spirits soar like the tenor of Cetera, our hearts soulful like the rasp of Kath, and our minds clear like the baritone of Lamm. And so to the only one who really knows what time it is, who brings us to that unending Saturday in the park—Father, Son, and Holy Spirit—be worship and praise, now and forever. *Amen.*

FOR BEFORE LISTENING TO RELIENT K

O Christ, who chose to be our escape from the rut in which we were stuck, be with us. When who we are hates who we've been, make these songs a reminder to come right out and say it, whereupon thou wilt take our heavy hearts and make them light. Help us to not gather regret for the things we can't change now; but rather to gather faith, that we might never underestimate our Jesus, who waited for us to be the ones thou wast waiting for, who reigns with the Father and the Holy Spirit, one God, in glory everlasting. *Amen.*

FOR BEFORE LISTENING TO KIRK FRANKLIN

O God our hero, who makes us want to stomp on death and the devil, thou art our life, our love, our all. Thou hast brought us to a brighter day and taught us melodies from heaven. Yet we have also been brought to the fight of our life, but by thy power we keep our heads to the sky, and we shout hosanna, for thou hast allowed us to imagine ourselves being free, trusting you totally. And before we get there, we will continue to lean on our Lord Jesus Christ—and oh there is something about that name—who reigns with the Father and the Holy Spirit, one God, revolution without end. *Amen.*

FOR BEFORE LISTENING TO JOHN MAYER

O God the heart of life, orient us. Whether we need thee to stop this train, or to aid us in moving on and getting over, be that which arrests us and which moves us. When gravity brings us down, and when we're dreaming with a broken heart, remind us there is no such thing as a "real world" in which thou art not sovereign and active. While we wait on this world to change, help us to trust ourselves with loving you. When we fail, help us to say what we need to say, that we may receive pardon and restoration. In our triumph, make us bold as the love of our Lord Jesus Christ, who reigns with the Father and the Holy Spirit, one God, now and forever. *Amen.*

FOR BEFORE LISTENING TO JAMES TAYLOR

O Christ, who showers the people you love with love, you are the secret o' life. You are the walking man who traversed city and country road to usher in the kingdom of God, that we might in turn shed a little light on this world. Help us to herald the Holy Spirit, for there is something in the way she moves, baptizing and cleansing with fire and rain. So when we go up on the roof to see the stars, or sing a song for you far away, don't let us be lonely tonight—show us your smiling face, and remind us we've got a friend in our Father, who reigns with you and the Holy Spirit, one God, world without end. *Amen.*

FOR BEFORE LISTENING TO NEEDTOBREATHE

O Spirit who washed us by the water, attend to us as we enter the soundscape of thy beloved Brothers Rinehart. Let the poetry sink deep into our souls like stones under rushing water. Let the notes be thine invitation to wake on up from our slumber, and testify that thou hast made us something beautiful. When we find ourselves to be the outsiders, be the crack in the door filled with light. When the devil's been talkin', make us bring our burdens and lay them down in the place only love can go, where our hallelujahs are multiplied unto our Brother who hath been our shelter—our Lord Jesus Christ, who reigns with thee and our Father, one God, world without end. *Amen.*

FOR BEFORE LISTENING TO THE OH HELLOS

O Christ, Soldier-Poet-King, attend to our ears, minds, and souls as we enter the soundscape of thy beloved Oh Hellos. In introspection, make us to say hello to our old hearts. If the truth be a cave, let us enter in, and whisper to us there in a voice so small. Like the dawn, be the light underneath which the shapes we knew change; by which we see the beauty in the way of things. Let us join in the choral anthems, and feel like children climbing trees. Whisper to us in the lullabies, that we may know who we are now. All this that we may see thy mercies in the blue hours of morning, and feel thy breath in the four winds, O Holy Spirit, who sings over us along with the Father and our Lord Jesus Christ, one God, world without end. *Amen.*

FOR BEFORE LISTENING TO JAMES BAY

O God the object of our craving, who held back the river that we might cross from death to life, we exalt thee. Could we give all we had, still our praise would remain incomplete, yet nonetheless thy love collides with our souls, and thus we move together. So when the sparks wane, and we live through scars, don't let the night slip through our hands. Rather remind us of when we were on fire, and, when we need the sun to break, send out thy light and let it go from thy heavenly seat to our hearts, which are no less the throne of our King Jesus Christ, who reigns with thee and the Holy Spirit, one God, world without end. *Amen.*

FOR BEFORE LISTENING TO CECE WINANS

O Heavenly Father, the I AM who has never failed us yet, we thirst for you. Your everlasting love brought us through life's trials to the healing part, where, welcomed into your throne room, we opened our alabaster box to pour out our love upon you. And because Mercy said no to the designs of the devil and the flesh, we can feel the Spirit moving like the wind upon our hearts, knowing that teardrops fall from heaven's eyes for each of our sorrows, and singing hallelujah to the king through both joy and pain, for he is a wonder—the Lover of our souls, Jesus Christ the holy Lamb, who reigns with you and the Holy Spirit, one God, now and forever. *Amen.*

FOR BEFORE LISTENING TO SANTANA

O Spirit in whom victory is won, who gave us your heart and made it real, it is by your design and salvation that life is for living. For when we were stuck in our evil ways, with no one to depend on, you called, "Maria, Maria," and through her assent to your will, you freed all the people. And one of these days your transcendence and immanence will be total in extent and degree, and the game of love will play on in endless progress as we are enraptured in our Lord Jesus Christ, who reigns with you and our Father, one God, world without end. *Amen.*

FOR BEFORE LISTENING TO GROVER WASHINGTON, JR.

O Christ, who spilled thy blood and let it flow over our sins, by thy redemption we are on the cusp of thine eternal reign. The poetry of thy word is the summer song which we sing as the winelight cascades over earth tones. The rhythm of thy grace is steady, for thou hast locked it in the pocket and set us to a soulful strut. And even now thou art building castles in the sky, which will descend to the new earth that we might one day go Santa Cruzin' with Mister Magic in paradise, who reigns with thee and the Holy Spirit, one God, now and forever. *Amen.*

FOR WHEN ONE'S JAM COMES ON

O Christ the Lamb, this is our jam. Thy governance over all random shuffles, streaming algorithms, and disc jockeys has lovingly delivered unto us this gift. So lift us now into a moment of rapturous ecstasy, as we shred air guitars as thou didst our sins, scream lyrics with the voice of the heavenly throng, and dance like Miriam when she dropped the hottest track of the thirteenth century BC. And as we lose it, wouldst thou use it for our blessing and that of those around us, and let us bring a smile or stank face to thee our Lord Jesus Christ, who reigns with our Father and the Holy Spirit, one God, in everlasting jubilation. *Amen.*

IX

CHURCH LIFE

WHEN I WAS at about the halfway point of my deconstruction-reconstruction journey during seminary, I made the decision to leave the conservative tradition in which I had been pursuing membership and ordination for about two years. As the dominoes of that decision started to fall, I remember feeling like I was throwing away all of the time, energy, and resources that I had invested in that space. I couldn't help but feel that I was burning bridges and letting people down—especially people who had sacrificially invested in me. It was easy to second-guess myself, thinking maybe I was just being fickle and consumeristic, looking for the mythical and illusive "perfect church" rather than hunkering down and committing to one tradition with its strengths and weaknesses.

But as I continued to pray and discern and talk it out with trusted advisors, I was able to more concretely project my potential future in the tradition I was leaving, and compare it against my future in the tradition I was considering entering. And as I did so, the loss I associated with leaving became less and less significant in contrast with what I'd be gaining. I remember reassuring myself, *This is not my attempt to find a way to avoid disagreement, tension, conflict, or personal unfulfillment in my vocation and in the church that I'm committing to. This is an attempt to follow the Holy Spirit as she leads me to a place where I can take up all of those crosses* without surrendering my integrity. *It's a struggle no matter what, but in what terrain can I struggle, and maybe even lose frequently, without losing* myself?

Integrity, for me, is about honoring my conscience as it speaks from a worldview that, to the best of my knowledge and hope, has come to me by God's direction and instruction as I have sought to know God's will and God's ways.

There was a time when it wouldn't have violated my conscience to see women prohibited from leadership, or LGBTQ folks excluded from the full sacramental life of the church, or social justice erased from the Gospel and the prophets; but there came a time when I couldn't exist in those spaces with integrity. And there was probably never a time when it wouldn't have violated my conscience to hear salvation taught in such a way that undermined genuine human free will and God's genuine desire and provision for all to be saved.

So it became clear: throwing in my lot with a tradition not only characterized but in fact defined by the above would be an act not of obedient self-giving, but rather of misguided self-destruction.

Thankfully, I had not only something to move away from, but also something to move toward. By God's providence I had found myself doing youth ministry during my first year of seminary at a wonderful Episcopal parish, which provided me the perfect on-ramp to the broader tradition. I set up a time to speak with the parish's vicar, in which we discussed the lay of the land and put together a plan by which I could assess whether the terrain of the Episcopal Church was that on which I could struggle in a sustainable way.

I worshipped repeatedly at four different parishes (ten times at some, hundreds of times at others) to get a sense of all the different ways to do Episcopal worship. I tried (and thankfully loved) the daily office as a normative form of Episcopal prayer. I took the intellectual freedom offered to me by a tradition whose unity is far more liturgical than confessional, and adopted a Molinist framework for creation, providence, and salvation. I became a member at a historically Black parish and learned many ways of integrating my expressions of Anglicanism and Blackness.

Don't get me wrong—the terrain is dry, rough, and even inhospitable in many places, marked by legacies of racism, moral therapeutic deism, elitism, and institutional atrophy. We're a church that in many ways (on the parishioner, parish, and diocesan levels) seems like it would rather die than be pruned by the Vinedresser to make room for new life.

But I believe this is the terrain on which I am to struggle. The ground on which I and many of my colleagues and friends are being uniquely equipped to cultivate new life.

I earnestly hope that you are in, or on your way to, a place and community of worship where you can exist with integrity. And terrain that is blooming in many spots, and ready for new life in its dead places. Wherever that may be.

FOR THOSE CHANGING TRADITIONS

O Bridegroom of the one, holy, catholic, and apostolic church, we commend to thy care those who have left one tradition and seek another to call home. Comfort us when we feel uprooted or dissociated, or that we are letting people down, or that our past is wasted. Whether we sojourn due to spiritual abuse, theological dissonance and change, or simply relocation, give us on-ramps to new traditions—people to guide us, and patient formation into new spiritualities. And bring us to resonance and integration through the great Builder who de- and reconstructs us—the Holy Spirit, who reigns with thee and our Father, one God, now and forever. *Amen.*

FOR WHEN ONE IS JUST VERY INTO THE IDEA OF THE ESCHATON

O Christ, whose consummated kingdom we eagerly anticipate, make the wonder of the advent of our final home ever fresh in our hearts and minds. Do kindly go ahead and reserve our time slots for sailing with Peter, songwriting with Hannah, big-cat-sitting with Daniel, chariot riding with Elijah, woodworking with Joseph, lyre lessons with David, tongue-speaking with the Eleven, and all other manner of perfect communion with the saints from across time and space. And help us to imagine going even further up and further in than this, by the illumination of the Holy Spirit, who reigns with thee and our Father, one God, in glory everlasting. *Amen.*

FOR INSTANCES OF SPIRITUAL ABUSE

O Christ our high priest, who reserves stricter judgment for church teachers, root out from thy beloved Bride all who abuse authority to bolster their privilege at the expense of others' God-given peace and power. Build up robust structures of church discipline for the reparation and prevention of emotional, sexual, or theological abuse, leaving no doubt that these acts disqualify one from leadership. Comfort and heal individuals and congregations who have been abused, and bring them, and all of us, leaders whose humility and accountability are infused with the Holy Spirit, who reigns with thee and our Father, one God, now and forever. *Amen.*

FOR DECHURCHED FOLKS

O Christ, cast out by the community of faith, we lift up those who have been hurt or disillusioned by the church. We lament and repent of what we have done, individually and structurally, to limit access to the life of the body. Pursue these thy beloved with steadfast care, and give them, perhaps through us, a new and blessed experience of godly community, where they are seen, valued, and empowered in the fullness of their being. And restore them to the household of the Father who celebrates them lavishly, reigning with thee and the Holy Spirit, one God, now and forever. *Amen.*

FOR THE CHURCH TO LOVE SINGLE FOLK WELL

O Christ, lover of our souls, we pray for thy holy church, that we may love our single siblings well. Use us to open up the avenues of attentive, devoted companionship that so often feel closed off to these thy beloved. Remind us that the friendship, not the family, is the basic unit of thy church. Teach us to recover our traditions of brother-making and sister-making, and help us to make and keep our vows to friends as solemnly as any others. Move upon married folk to invite single folk into their domestic rhythms. Move upon church leaders to create a culture and infrastructure of intentional community. For thou hast fashioned us with a deep need for community, which is made possible through our Lord Jesus Christ, who reigns with thee and the Holy Spirit, one God, world without end. *Amen.*

FOR THEOLOGICAL DISAGREEMENT

O God of wisdom, sovereign over the polyphony of theologies in thy holy Scriptures and in thy church across time and space, we praise thee for thy gracious accommodation to our limited perspectives. Do incline thine ear as we lift up to thee our relationships with those with whom our beliefs are opposed. Give us strong convictions, but also open minds. Keep us from making our theologies sources of pride, self-righteousness, or disengagement. Rather allow respectful conflict to open us up and deepen our knowledge of one another. And as thou didst with Peter's vision, show us when our beliefs are out of step with the Holy Spirit, who guides us into all truth through our Lord Jesus Christ, in the love of the Father, one God, world without end. *Amen*.

FOR SPIRITUAL MOTHERS

O Mother God, God of Junia, Priscilla, and Mary of Magdala, we thank thee for the women thou hast called, equipped, and installed as our spiritual mothers. By thy providence they have been, and are now, and will continue to be indispensable to the integrity and work of thy church. Undermine and eradicate the patriarchalism and sexism against which they must strive, and cultivate in us a reverence and sweet filial affection for them. For great is the company of women who bear the tidings of our Lord Jesus Christ, who reigns with thee and the Holy Spirit, one God, now and forever. *Amen*.

FOR A NEWLY ORDAINED PERSON

O Head of the Church, we revel in thy calling, equipping, and ordination of [name] to the presbyterate. In the spring of their ministry, channel their youthful passion and ingenuity to challenge thy church. In the summer of their ministry, give them the staying power of a dependable shepherd. In the autumn of their ministry, equip them to train and mentor young presbyters and sister churches. And in the winter of their ministry, let them, like Simeon, depart from the sanctuary in peace upon seeing thy glory revealed, and enter the arms of Jesus Christ, the acclaim of the Father, and the delight of the Holy Spirit, one God, world without end. *Amen*.

FOR CHURCHES IN TRANSITION

O Lord of each and every season, mainsail in all seas, we approach thee on behalf of parishes facing transition and needing renewal. Help these congregations name and mourn that which we have lost. Show us those factors in our decline which are out of our control, and those which are within, and how to adapt. Where leadership vacuums exist, bring capable and Spirit-led interim and permanent leaders—lay and clergy. And make us play a redemptive role in the ecology of the place thou hast given us to inhabit, serve, and love for the sake of our Lord Jesus Christ, who reigns with thee and the Holy Spirit, one God, world without end. *Amen.*

FOR CHURCH PLANTERS AND REVITALIZERS

O Sower of seed, who raises up new communities, we pray thy power upon church planters. Graciously continue to give them imagination and innovative spirit. Give them freedom to take risks and lead in the unknown, even at the cost of our discomfort. May they be supported abundantly, by funds, structures, laity, and clergy. May they discern what to uproot, what to nurture, and how to slowly restore the health of the soil. And make their churches unified internally and effective outwardly, for the love and edification of their neighborhoods and the revealing of the glory of our Lord Jesus Christ, who lives and reigns with thee and the Holy Spirit, one God, now and forever. *Amen.*

FOR THOSE PURSUING ORDINATION

O Father who trains us up in the way we should go, who calls the unworthy and equips the called, we entrust all candidates for ordination to thy guidance. Remind us daily of our inward and outward call. Form us to meet the needs of thy church. Like David keeping sheep, make our time of preparation a time of listening, testing, and steady faithfulness, that we may be ready to be entrusted with more. Make the process transparent, red tape minimal, and bishops and ordaining bodies supportive. And let our theology always be controlled by our doxology, as we respond in worship to the call of our Lord Jesus Christ, who reigns with thee and the Holy Spirit, one God, world without end. *Amen.*

FOR BIPOC AT WHITE AND MULTIETHNIC CHURCHES

O Christ, great and greatly to be praised in every cultural expression, shepherd people of color who are members of white churches. Whether overtly or subtly racist, tokenistic or quietist, or hopefully anti-racist, make plain the cultural competency of their church. If thou wouldst have them leave, shake the dust off their feet, console them through the pain, and lead them to a new home. If not, construct a healthy and equitable way to remain put, ensuring that their experience is centered, normalized, and dignified for what it is—the glorious provision of our Mother who reigns with thee and the Holy Spirit, one God, now and forever. *Amen.*

FOR OUTDOOR WORSHIP

O God who makes the whole world your temple, just as you have consecrated our sanctuaries, make the place where we are standing holy ground. In the absence of the human adornments of the chapel, make the grass, the air, the light, the sky, and sights and sounds of town into signs of your glory and enrichments of our worship. Send forth the sights and sounds of our praise as a witness to our neighbors; a symbol of the ongoing expansion of the love, hospitality, and sacred space of the Holy Spirit, who reigns with you and our Savior Jesus Christ, one God, now and forever. *Amen.*

FOR WORSHIP LED BY KIDS

O God whose kingdom belongs to children and the childlike, who brings forth wisdom from the mouth of babes, lead us in worship through the work, words, and wonder of the youngest of our church family. Help us to rediscover even for a moment their way of seeing the world, that we might come with an honest and open heart to your tender parental embrace, through Jesus Christ the child who taught the teachers, who reigns with you and the Holy Spirit, one God, now and forever. *Amen.*

FOR CHURCH REVIVAL

O Holy Spirit, the divine breath which fills our lungs and fans the flames of revival, give us expectant hearts to receive visions of renewal in and through thy church; pour them into us like endless oil into open vessels. Call us daily to the quiet altar to hear—and to the public square to proclaim—words which align with the dreams gestating in the souls of the faithful, the devotion modeled by the greatest saints, and the structures being reformed by the hand of our Lord Jesus Christ, who reigns with thee and our Father, one God, now and forever. *Amen.*

FOR THE ROAD TO EMMAUS

O Christ, who often comes upon us unawares, accompanying us in ways that we do not yet perceive, come alongside us. Make our hearts and lips forthright, that we might testify to our despair, even while unaware of the fullness of your presence; that you might reframe the evidence around us with ancient and present truth. Stay with us until we see your story—until we see you, who sets our hearts ablaze with the fire of the Holy Spirit and of the I AM, one God, now and forever. *Amen.*

FOR NEW WINE AND NEW WINESKINS

O Spirit who reveals the gospel and its implications afresh for each generation, make us firm in our convictions yet soft in our receptiveness to new forms of faithfulness. Put in our lives those who, by taking space and bearing witness, help us to weave new wineskins; and like new wine, pour new relationships and new wisdom into the vessels you've made and refashioned, that through us the Spirit might not quench but rather overflow, poured out from the self-emptied Christ, who reigns with you and our Potter, one God, now and forever. *Amen.*

FOR TRANSFIGURATION

O God who speaks in sheer sound of silence, give us respite from the noise of chaos. Bring us to the mountain, that we might glimpse your glory, and have what lies below illuminated by that same radiance. Transfigure yourself before us, and give us those with whom to witness and be transformed. Hasten the time when the mysteries with which we've been nourished will gain the ears of our siblings who have yet to see what we've seen revealed by the Holy Spirit, who reigns with you and our Savior Jesus Christ, one God, in glory everlasting. *Amen.*

FOR WRESTLING WITH GOD

O God who speaks out of the whirlwind, heal our limbs which have been ripped apart by the strain between our knowledge of your character and our perception of your action or inaction in the world. You have given us faith to seek understanding, so help us to integrate what we know to be true with what is happening in front of us. Bring us friends who tag in when we can't wrestle with you any longer. And when our wrestling leaves us with a limp, leave us also with a new identity and new understanding of the ongoing presence of Christ, who reigns with you and the Holy Spirit, one God, now and forever. *Amen.*

BENEDICTION

THANK YOU FOR reading. Thank you for praying these prayers with me. Thank you for supporting this work and the work of creating new liturgical resources for the church. I hope these collects can supplement the liturgies—however formal or informal—of your church services, Bible studies, meditations, blogs, family devotionals, and other spaces of prayer. If you have a story regarding how anything in this book has inspired you, I'd love to hear it (feel free to reach out on Instagram or on my website).

And now—

May God draw your life ever more into the perfect life of the Trinity.

May God teach you a life of prayer that gathers up every experience, especially those often seen to be out of prayer's reach, and lays them on the altar in anticipation of God's sacramental reception and reframing.

May God lead you to new forms of faithfulness and devotion that, like the walls and rooms of a home, though unchanging in structure, grow in significance alongside the meaning that is made inside of them.

May God guide you to plumb the depths of the riches of our tradition, in all its varied expressions and communions, finding ways to stand on the shoulders of the matriarchs and patriarchs, the prophets, the poets, the apostles, the early mothers and fathers, the martyrs, the monastics, the scholastics, the reformers, the moderns, the contemporaries.

May God bring overlooked, underutilized, or even new forms of prayer out of your searching for these riches.

May God show you prayers that express what you were feeling but couldn't yet articulate.

May God reveal God's deep care and attentiveness to all the things you didn't know you could or should pray about.

May God console you, may God affirm you, may God shepherd you, may God delight you out of the inexhaustible stores of divine love and joy.

In everything, by prayer and supplication with thanksgiving, let your requests be made known to God. And the peace of God, which surpasses all understanding, will guard your hearts and your minds in Christ Jesus.

In the name of the Father, Son, and Holy Spirit; Mother, Daughter, Holy Ghost; Creator, Redeemer, Sustainer; Progenitor, Progeny, and Procession. *Amen.*

ACKNOWLEDGMENTS

JACLYN, THANK YOU for supporting this project from the very beginning, buoying me with your enthusiasm and opening my eyes to all the different places it could go.

Ekemini, thank you for opening doors to publishing, promoting my work, convincing me to start an Instagram page, giving feedback on countless collects, and most importantly, befriending me.

Ashley, thank you for taking publication from a vague idea to a very present reality, from altruistically giving me advice and agent contacts, to perfectly capturing and advocating for the concept and value of my work, to being the best editor a guy could ask for.

Weird Christian Twitter and especially Weird Anglican Twitter (esp. Adam, Mtr. Kara, Mtr. Joyce, Fr. Cody, Fr. David, and Kara), thank you for the support that turned this from a one-off tweet into a series of tweets and off to the races from there.

Rachelle, for grasping and furthering my vision, for opening doors, for giving the perfect balance of freedom and guidance, and for your patient work of cultivating this seed all the way through to this harvest.

June and Terry, for raising me up in the way I should go.

Ben and John Paul, Sang and Charmain, Isaac, Dennis, DJ, Russ, Mika, Fr. Lee, Mtr. Christine, Joel, Bijan, Seth, Stephanie, and Amos, for leading me into the arms of Love.

SPACE FOR YOUR
OWN WRITTEN COLLECTS

THIS COLLECT "RECIPE" has enriched my prayer life; I hope this will encourage and prompt you to try the spiritual practice of prayer-writing for yourself in these pages:

1. Pick a title—what or who the prayer is for.
2. Begin the prayer with an address to God.
3. Continue with an attribute or action of God.
4. Craft some content—what do you want to say to God about this?
5. End with a Trinitarian doxology.

ABOUT THE AUTHOR

TERRY J. STOKES is the associate pastor of youth and community engagement at the Reformed Church of Highland Park, in New Jersey. He weaves together his experience in several church contexts with his theological education, his knowledge of pop culture, and his devotional life to write prayers that encourage the heart of today's church.